Dec '91.

Angus /

many thanks for the disco at our Group 'do'. It was enjoyed and appreciated by all and helped make it an evening to remember

Kind Regards and Best Wishes

John Gunton (and all the Wroe Group)

Blue Coat

A History of the Blue Coat School
Birmingham
1722 – 1990

by
John D. Myhill

Meridian Books

(in association with the Blue Coat School, Birmingham)

Published 1991 by Meridian Books in association with the Blue Coat School, Birmingham.

© John D. Myhill 1991

ISBN 1-869922-14-X

Meridian Books
40 Hadzor Road
Oldbury
Warley
West Midlands
B68 9LA

Printed in Great Britain by BPCC Wheatons Ltd., Exeter.

Contents

Illustrations

Preface

In 1961 I moved to Birmingham to become Housemaster of St. Philip's House at the Blue Coat School and left two years later to take up an overseas appointment. Soon after joining the school I realised that no one could answer my questions about the rather unusual history of its foundation and growth so I decided to look into this myself and find the answers to my questions. This led me quite quickly to the aim of writing a brief history of the school and absorbed all my free time over the two years.

Just before leaving the school, I managed to complete the work and had three copies typed. One copy went to the school Governors, one to the City Reference Library and the third, together with all the documents and correspondence that had accumulated, went into a drawer of my desk and stayed there, more or less overlooked, for more than twenty years. At that point I decided to use some of the material for a talk I was giving locally and was disappointed to find that some of the illustrations I had intended to include were not attached to my typescript copy.

In the hope of rectifying this situation I got in touch with the Reference Library and the School. The Reference Library, which had meanwhile changed its site, had a microfilm copy (though this was later found to be incomplete) but no typescript copy or illustrations and the School copy could not be traced.

I felt compelled to do something to make sure that the story of the School, of those who founded it and nurtured its well-being for nearly three hundred years should be available to anyone interested. The result is this book, a fragment of local history, dedicated to the generosity and compassion of many Birmingham citizens and to all Blue Coat boys and girls, past, present and future.

J. D. Myhill

Introduction

In writing this account of the School's history, I have intended to bring together in one volume the facts recorded in various documents, not all of which are readily available to those interested in the School, and which furthermore are not deposited centrally. A number of these documents and references may be consulted in the City Reference Library. The most interesting of them, as a financial and statistical record, is a booklet published in 1784 with the title *An Historical Account of the Blue Coat Charity School, Birmingham, from its institution in 1724 to 1784*. This booklet was reprinted and brought up to date in 1806, 1817 and 1830. The contents of all four issues are almost identical.

Further documentary information was found in the Cathedral records, in the Diocesan Registry records, and in the Bodleian Library, Oxford. All these sources are listed in an Appendix. By far the most important records however, are the Minute Books of the General Committee, now constituted as the Governing Body of the School. With the exception of two missing volumes covering the years 1773 – 1780 and 1795 – 1802, these books provide a complete record of the resolutions of the Governing Body for the 267 years of the School's existence. All these books have been kept in good condition and were, of course, held by the School.

Very recently they have been moved on permanent loan to the Archives Department of the Central Reference Library, Birmingham and eventually will be available to the public for reference. They are interesting documents from many points of view but not light fare. Eighteenth and nineteenth century handwriting varied from exquisite penmanship, of which two examples are reproduced in this book, to closely written and untrained writing which is difficult to follow. Readers will find some variations in spelling as well as some unusual sentence constructions in the extracts from these books. I have left these in their original form rather than modernise or standardise them.

The story gathered from these various sources is a part of local history. It is unfortunately true that the story is known to few people apart from former scholars and their families, and those persons who have been connected officially with the School. I felt it should be better known. A small group of citizens, spurred by their consciences, tackled a social problem from their own resources. It has been my privilege to record their work and their names.

I am keenly aware that not all those who gave services or financial support to the School during its long existence, have been mentioned in this book. Although my work in preparing the material convinced me that none of these people wished for public recognition of their generosity, I would like to express my regret that it has not been possible to mention them all by name.

Lastly, I wanted the records to speak for themselves whenever possible. This method has given to the story the authenticity and authority of recorded facts. It has, I realise, the drawback that many sections consist of a long series of small and sometimes disconnected items which give a textbook appearance. I could see no way of avoiding this format and hope that it will not discourage the reader.

"The worst sin towards our fellow creatures is not to hate them, but to be indifferent to them; that's the essence of inhumanity."

G. B. Shaw. *The Devil's Disciple.*

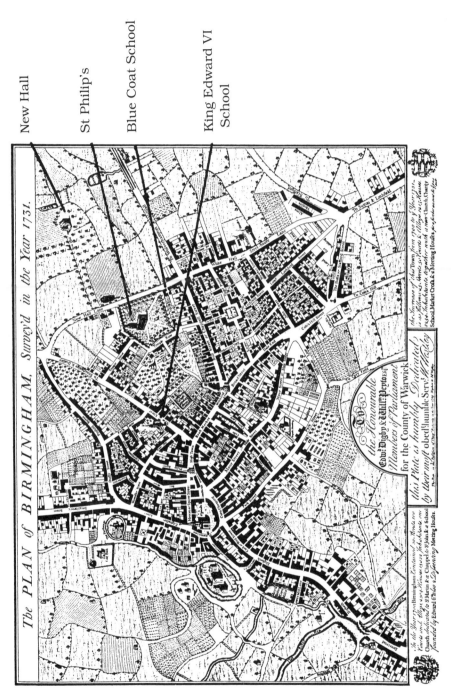

New Hall

St Philip's

Blue Coat School

King Edward VI School

The PLAN of BIRMINGHAM, Survey'd in the Year 1731.

Wm. Westley's Plan of Birmingham surveyed in 1731.

1

The School is Needed

The newly built church of St. Philip's had been completed and consecrated in 1715 by Edward, Bishop of Lichfield and Coventry, and the first rector, The Reverend William Higgs, had moved into the new Parsonage House. The church stood proudly on a pleasant, open site in the district then referred to as the High Town. In his *History of Birmingham*, published in 1819, Hutton wrote of it:

> "When I first saw St. Philip's at a proper distance, uncrowded with houses, for there were none to the North, New Hall excepted, untarnished by smoke and illuminated by a western sun, I was delighted with its appearance and thought it then, what I do now and what others will in future, the pride of the place. If we assemble the beauties of the edifice which cover a rood of ground, the spacious area of the churchyard, occupying four acres, ornamented with walks in great perfection, shaded with trees in double and treble ranks, and surrounded with buildings in elegant taste, perhaps its equal cannot be found in the British Dominions."

On the lower South side, extending from Temple Row to within a few yards of New Street and the Free Grammar School of King Edward VI was the cherry orchard known as Walker's Cherry Orchard. The present Cherry Street occupies part of this ground.

Few buildings interrupted the further view, on the other side of New Street, of Greenwood's Cherry Orchard and an area of gardens. Looking North from the church, green meadows sloped down what is now the area of Snow Hill to the Little Pool and the Great Pool at the foot of the hill. The only building in this rural scene was the imposing house known as New Hall, approached by a long, tree lined avenue leading off New Hall Lane, the modern Colmore Row.

The Church Commissioners who had been appointed to establish a new parish church for the growing township, could afford to be well satisfied with their choice of site and with the magnificent church, towards the cost of which £600 had been subscribed by King George I in 1709. Previously known as the Horse Close, the site had been bought from a Mrs. Elizabeth Phillips, widow of Robert Phillips, and was sufficiently extensive to leave over, after the requirements of the Church, the churchyard and the Parsonage House had been met, an area of land on the east side of the church, for which the Commissioners had no immediate use. This possibility had been foreseen when the site was bought, for in the Act of 1709, authorising the establishment of the new parish, it was stated:

> "The said Commissioners . . . may dispose of the remainder of the said Close, after the Church built and the Churchyard set out as aforesaid, as they shall think most for the advantage of the Rector."

This surplus area of land and the discretionary powers allowed to the Commissioners for its eventual use were to be of great importance in making possible the establishment of the Blue Coat Charity School, only a few years later. The ground was referred to in 1722 as:

> "A little piece of ground not yet made use of, that is to say from the lane leading from Bull Street in Birmingham aforesaid to or towards New Hall up to a stake or mark which is within five yards of the garden wall belonging to the said Parsonage House."

There was no urgency however, in 1715, to use the land, and presumably the Reverend William Higgs was more concerned with his duties and problems as Rector of the new parish, to give the matter much of his time. Furthermore, as he looked out from the Parsonage House across the hundreds of acres of open land that stretched to the North from New Hall Lane, the 'little piece of ground' must have seemed a relatively unimportant asset. His first care no doubt would be to become acquainted with his parishioners and through them to learn more about the community of which he was now a part.

Among those who would soon have established themselves as leading members of the new church were many influential citizens of this growing town; men who held office as Constable of the Town, as Overseer of the Poor, as Churchwardens; merchants and tradesmen whose initiative and energy were building the reputation of the town. From them, and by personal observation, the new Rector would soon have learned how this community of 20,000 people lived and worked. There was indeed much to be pleased with. The town was rapidly becoming one of the important manufacturing centres of England, known widely for the brass, iron, leather, buttons, jewellery, thread and tools which it supplied to the markets of the country. Yet there were no grimy factories, all the work being undertaken in the artisans' own homes or in small adjacent outbuildings. Consequently, as we can see from the 1731 map by William Westley, the citizens enjoyed a natural setting of uncrowded lanes, grazed meadows and open views.

Inside this agreeable setting not all was well however. There were many circumstances to concern men who had a conscience and a perception of social and moral justice. The most compelling of these was the appalling though accepted neglect suffered by the children of the poor, a neglect which was perhaps begun in the home but was certainly sealed by local and national indifference to their conditions of life. Few, if any indeed, attended school, for there was no school system to provide for them. Langford wrote in his *Century of Birmingham Life*:

"The references to education which we find in the old papers are, like angels' visits, few and far between. There was no thought then of popular education. It was deemed dangerous to teach people too much. In the cant of the day it unfitted them for their stations and made them discontented in the situation in which God had placed them."

It was not until 150 years later, that education for all became the law of the land. In the Birmingham of 1715, education was provided at the Free Grammar School of King Edward VI in New Street, and in a few small proprietary establishments for a very small percentage of the total of children; in fact only the poor, untaught and unconsidered, were left to chase through the streets and alleys until they were thought old enough to be put to work. Their freedom was brief, for the majority of them, untrained for life, illiterate and physically immature, began their working days at the age of nine. A Royal Commission report of this time stated:

"Cases have occurred of children staying from eight in the morning till seven at night without food . . . If the men did not sometimes help them by giving them part of their own dinners, they would have scarcely anything to eat . . . They are generally badly clothed, the best part of this shop have neither shoes nor stockings, winter or summer."

Authentic figures for this period are not available. A hundred and twenty years later however, in 1844, of the 23,000 children under the age of fifteen years in Birmingham, half were not receiving any instruction within the Borough, and about a quarter

of this number went to Sunday School only. The report added
that:

> "The majority of the children in the Birmingham district
> commence work before they are nine years of age."

As with education, so with their moral well being. They received
little or no guidance. Early eighteenth century England had yet
to be scourged by the crusading Wesleys and meanwhile the
young generation was required to make what it could of the
environment in which it lived.

It is a fairly safe conjecture that these matters had been causing
concern to many of the town's leading citizens, particularly to
those of them who were church members, for some time. As the
population grew, the problem became more evident, and from
being the subject of casual conversation, no doubt became the
main topic of meetings, arranged in order to find an answer to a
state of affairs that discredited the community. Also there was
one other problem, this time not a social one, that must have been
discussed frequently. A strong dissenting body was appearing in
the town. 'The Several Dissenters' places of worship marked on
the 1731 plan, such as the Old and New Meeting Houses and the
Baptists' Meeting House, are evidence of the growing number of
Nonconformists among the inhabitants of the town. Later in the
century the friction between this body of Nonconformists and the
supporters of the Anglican Church, would lead to riots and
violence in which the New Meeting House was razed to the ground.
Also razed was the home of Dr. Priestley, the eminent scientist
and the town's most distinguished and outspoken Nonconformist. Feeling had not reached this explosive level in the early years
of St. Philip's but the growing strength of this rival to the
established church would already have become a topic for serious
discussion among the Anglican clergy of the town and the influential members of the vestries and congregations.

These circumstances, the illiterate condition of most of the
town's children, the lack of moral guidance available to them, and
the increasing influence of the Nonconformist elements in the
town caused sufficient concern to lead from general discussion
to a particular proposal for tackling these problems. The proposal
was to found a Charity School, closely linked with the established
Church.

2

The School is Founded

It would be satisfying to present at this point a factual record of the origin of the proposal and of the practical steps taken to secure support and to raise the money needed. No such record is available and it is unlikely that any was ever made. The proposal was to do something practical and useful. Writing a record of events would not appeal to practical men unless they were obliged to do so by legal requirements. This attitude of doing things, rather than of writing about doing things, remained a characteristic of the school's management. It has however made impossible the verification of many facts, not least being the course of events about the year 1720, for the scheme must have been taking shape then, to allow of the building being started in 1722.

Various possibilities are well worth consideration. Charitable foundations had been set up in many parts of the country, the best known being Christ's Hospital founded in 1552 in the reign of King Edward VI. Reports of these Charity Schools and the work they were doing would have been brought to the town, if by no one else, then by members of the clergy. The Society for the Propagation of Christian Knowledge, which had received Royal assent in 1701, had promoted this movement in many districts and the influence of the Society may have led to the adoption of the scheme in Birmingham. This possibility is made stronger by the fact that Dr. Bray, one of the founders of the S.P.C.K. held the living at Sheldon from 1690 onwards, under the patronage of Lord Digby. Digby was one of the Commissioners, no doubt the most influential, who had supervised the building of St. Philip's Church. Given his support of the idea of a Charity School, and his support of the lease of the 'little piece of land' adjacent to the churchyard for the School, the proposal would have had powerful backing. It is a possibility then that Lord Digby as Church Commissioner and Dr. Bray as a leading member of the S.P.C.K. were the original sponsors, with the Reverend Higgs as a willing ally.

These may have been the men responsible for urging the idea and for offering support, but the realisation of the proposal was certainly delegated to others, who had a greater knowledge of local matters and a more immediate concern with local conditions. A near neighbour of Dr. Bray was Dr. Richard Banner, minister of Marston Chapel. Banner was a native of Birmingham, born there in 1680, son of Sam Banner, ironmonger. Educated at King Edward VI School in New Street and at University College, Oxford, he was ordained in 1702 and appointed to the newly consecrated chapel in Marston in 1704. This was to be his only preferment, and his involvement with the affairs of the town during the next thirty years is evidenced by the several positions he held. At various times he was Churchwarden of St. Philip's, Constable of the Town (one of two), and a member of the governing body of the Workhouse.

Dr. Banner's role in the founding of the school was important but limited to one task. His signature heads the list of signatories to the lease of the land from St. Philip's in 1722. It seems likely that he undertook the work of negotiating the lease on behalf of a body which required of him this one service. He was chosen for this work, no doubt, on the grounds of being a clergyman, also because he was known to all the parties concerned, and perhaps, because since the publication of his *Treatise on Simony* in 1716, he had gained a reputation for knowledge of legal matters. Among the names of the subscribers at the first committee meeting to consider the building of the School was that of the Reverend John Banner, his brother. Since Sam Banner, the father of Richard and John, was churchwarden of St. Philip's in 1720, and later was also a member of the School Committee, all three played parts of varying significance in the story of the school's establishment.

The Banner family was connected by marriage with the Vaughton family, which had settled in Birmingham in the reign of Queen Elizabeth. The Vaughtons had prospered in business, acquiring land in many districts of the town and in the immediate vicinity. At this time, Riland Vaughton was a man of considerable wealth. He gave generously to several causes in the town, including a sum of £500 towards the completion of the tower of St. Philip's.

To the proposed Charity School, he bequested in 1722, a like amount — £500. He died in the same year, at the early age of 34, while the school was still little more than an idea, as far as can be ascertained the first benefactor of the school. Riland Vaughton was a relative by marriage of Thomas Guy, founder of Guy's Hospital. This alliance may well have inspired him to make this generous donation.

Such are the facts behind the establishment of the school. They indicate strongly that several Birmingham families, related by marriage and closely linked with the Church, the Church authorities themselves, and possibly the S.P.C.K, through Dr. Bray, were the most influential elements of the movement to found the school, providing between them influence and money, while delegating to others the practical details involved in opening and managing the school.

The first requisite, to provide a suitable location, was met in November 1722, when the "small piece of land" was formally leased by the Church authorities to the managing body of the proposed school. Dated 6th November 1722, the indenture of lease set out that the Church Commissioners (appointed for building the church of St. Philip and making the new parish) together with Edward, Lord Bishop of Coventry and Lichfield, and the Rector of St. Philip's, the Reverend William Higgs, granted to Richard Banner and ten others, inhabitants of Birmingham, this piece of land on which to build a school. The land was leased for a period of 1,000 years at an annual rental of ten shillings, payable to the Rector of the parish. This document confirmed legally an agreement already made, since in referring to the land there is a statement:

"Upon part whereof a Charity School is now building".

This situation is substantiated by the School Order Book, in which the first entry, dated August 10th 1722 (three months before the formal signing of the lease) consists of a building programme. Evidently there was then a fine disregard for the legalities that have since imposed themselves upon the conduct of our affairs, and a commendable belief in the honouring of verbal agreements. As in this case, land was often conveyed after building on it had started, even after completion of the building work.

The leasehold terms agreed between the various parties were of negligible advantage to the Reverend William Higgs and to his successors as Rector of St. Philip's. The rental charged was a nominal amount, 50*p.* in modern currency, entirely unrelated to the value of the land and fixed at the lowest figure possible to give the transaction legal authority. It denied any intention on the part of the Church authorities to profit from the concession of the land. On the contrary, their proposal of such terms emphasised the complete identification of the Church with the project and a willingness therefore to forego any advantage that could have been derived, in order to avoid putting any financial strain on the young institution. This generous approach conferred a benefit on the school that was not only immediate but was to grow hugely in value as land prices rose steeply in the fast growing town.

A significant feature of this curious document is the inclusion of a lengthy explanation of the reasons for founding the school.

> "Profaneness and debauchery are greatly owing to a gross ignorance of the Christian Religion, especially among the poorer sort; and that nothing is more likely to promote the practice of Christianity than an early and pious education of youth."

The land was leased:

> "From the 29th day of September, 1722, for the uses of a School to be built thereon, for the purpose of maintaining poor children, teaching them to read and write, and instructing them in the knowledge of the Christian religion, as professed in the Church of England; and for other purposes."

The inclusion of these statements in a document that had as its main purpose the legalising of a land transaction provides further evidence of the identity of views of the Church authorities and of the School's promoters. Non-conformism was repudiated. In fact the two parties were a division of one body. Those granting the lease were the representatives of the church; the eleven leaseholders were prominent officials and supporters of the church. It was stipulated in the document that the eleven trustees, when reduced to four by death or removal, were to appoint seven others, being residents of Birmingham who subscribed annually not less than one guinea to the Charity. Their signatures to the document appear in the following order.

1.   Richard Banner — Clerk
2.   Charles Blackham
3.   William Wheeley
4.   Henry Carver
5.   John Sale
6.   Walter Tippin
7.   Nehemiah Tonkes
8.   John Porter
9.   Robert Fullwood
10.   John Cottrell
11.   Robert Johnson

The known facts about the Reverend Dr. Richard Banner have been given already. Of the other ten, most of what is known consists of their connection with St. Philip's. After the church was consecrated, the first Churchwardens to be appointed on 5th October 1715, were Henry Carver and John Cottrell. Their names and signatures appear in the Vestry records of St. Philip's on several later dates when they were re-appointed as Church-wardens or were signatories to the records. The same is true of Nehemiah Tonkes, William Wheeley and Walter Tippin.

It may well be that this list is a roll of the founders, for when the time had come that the first suggestions had hardened into practical moves, when plans had developed into realities, and this important legal transaction was being finalised, surely the men who put their names to this document would be those who had inspired the idea. This possibility is strengthened by the following extract from the *Historical Account of the Blue Coat School 1724 – 1784.*

"In the year 1773 the following persons were appointed trustees by the late Mr. Thomas Tippin of Wilton, sole executor of <u>Mr. Walter Tippin, the last trustee</u> . . . "

Some caution is necessary however before accepting totally this surmise. The term 'founder' was nowhere mentioned; only the words 'trustees' and 'subscribers' were used in the records. All the indications are that those who had worked to establish the school were doing what they thought was right and necessary and sought no personal acclaim or public recognition. However pompous the style of the documents and records they left behind, it is beyond doubt that the founders and first subscribers were modest to the point of self effacement and anonymity. Otherwise we would be able to identify them more readily. This is an aspect moreover, of the school's management that has persisted throughout. Possibly then, behind those who put their signatures to this document, were others whose work has not been recorded. Also, the signing of this lease was not the first move towards the establishment of the school. The building itself had already been started, and the authorisation for this work had been given, as we shall see, by a body of men of whom only two had signed the land lease.

Signatures on the 1722 land lease.

3

The School is Built

"It is this tenth day of August 1722 agreed by and between the subscribers of the Charity School in Birmingham in the county of Warwickshire, whose names are hereunto put on the one part and Samuel Avery of the parish of St. Philip's in Birmingham aforesaid, Bricklayer on the other part. This is to say that the said Samuel Avery doth hereby promise and agree to and with the said subscribers to erect and build a paire of building adjoining to St. Philip's Churchyard in Birmingham aforesaid, for the Schooling and Education of poor children in Birmingham and to finish and complete the same firm and substantial in every part, and to lay all and every bricks and tiles that are to be used in the said building at three shillings a thousand and also to do and finish all and every his said work on or before the thirtieth day of November next. And the subscribers do promise and agree to and with the said Samuel Avery to provide for and find at their own costs and charges all and every the bricks, tiles, lime, lath and lath nails for the said pair of building and to lay down the same in some convenient place near where these buildings are to be erected and in due convenient time. And also pay the said Samuel Avery 3s. a thousand for laying the bricks and tiles as aforesaid. In witness whereof the parties above mentioned have hereunto put their hands the day and year above."

Subscribers present:
Tho. Duncombe   Sam Avery
Nehemiah Tonkes
Charles Blackham
Joshua Lowe
Ed. Ward
Nicholas Silvester
John Banner
Ed. Allison
Tho. Wood

This formal contract is the first entry in the Minute Books. Stripped of the "aforesaids" and a little overlay of legal phraseology, it is a remarkably simple and straightforward agreement, offering yet another insight into the unsophisticated and uncomplicated approach to business matters at this time, as well as illustrating the inconsistencies of spelling and grammar characteristic of much eighteenth century writing. More paperwork would be needed today to buy a few shares in British Gas. Samuel Avery, bricklayer, was a member of the vestry of St. Philip's and so was Joshua Lowe. Tho. Duncombe was the proprietor of the Swan Inn. Of the others only Charles Blackham and Nehemiah Tonkes were signatories to the land lease, later in the year.

Following this first entry, a meeting held twelve weeks later on November 2nd 1722 set out:

1) Orders to be observed by the Master and Mistress in the Government of the Charity Schools in Birmingham.

2) Rules to be observed by the Trustees and Subscribers to the Charity Schools in Birmingham.

Both these documents are reproduced in the appendices. Just one week later, on November 9th, a similar agreement to that made with Samuel A ˄ry, was recorded as having been concluded with Thomas Land the Elder and with William Westley[*] for the carpentry work. The signatures are the same as those on the 10th August agreement, with the addition of that of Samuel Avery. There now occurs a period of several months before the subscribers had further business to attend to. A 'Solemn Meeting' on the 1st March 1723 ordered that:

"The Charity Schoole shall be finished out of the money now in the Treasurer's hands or out of what shall be collected in such manner as the Revd. Mr. Banner, Mr. Blackham, Mr. Wheeley, Mr. Tippin, Mr. Duncombe, Mr. John Porter and Mr. Tonkes or the major part of them shall think fitt."

Then in May of 1723 there was a renewal of activity. Thomas Duncombe who was obviously acting as Treasurer, was ordered

---

[*] This is very likely to be the same Westley who produced the 1731 plan of St. Philip's church. In *Memorials of the Old Square, 1897* is the assertion: "That Westley was a considerable sharer in the building transactions is shown by the accommodation road known in later years as the Coach Yard and London Prentice Street, being originally named Westley's Row". Later still it was renamed Dalton Street.

to buy boards for flooring the school and to pay 'the workmen their bills'. On the same date a clothing order was placed with John Millington and others. The order consisted of:

> "Three and thirty pairs of leather breeches after the rate of 8*d.* a pair and a shilling over for the whole. Six and thirty coats and waistcoats for the boys and 14 gowns and petty-coats for the girles — 20*d.* for the boys coats and waistcoats and 12*d.* for the girles gowns and pettycoats". Also "50 pairs of shoes for the boys and girles at 22*d.* per pair".

The meeting of June 14th of the same year laid down very firmly that subscribers should meet on every Tuesday at 6 p.m. to transact affairs and that no business should be done after eight o'clock. All this firmness had a very human sequel as the next meeting appears to have been held on September 17th when it was ordered that the cellar stairs should be of brick, not timber, and then there is a gap until a meeting on March 31st 1724. It is possible of course that the Order Book was not used to record deliberations and that during these lengthy intervals no decisions were made or recorded, although regular meetings were held.

There appear to have been two regular meeting places at this time, when no school accommodation was ready. One was the Swan Inn in Edmund Street, kept by Thomas Duncombe, which in 1731 became the starting point of the stage coach for London; the other was the Castle Inn, Lancaster Place. It was in one of these Inns that the subscribers decided on May 19th to order bedsteads and flocks to be made, to pay Mr. Samuel Avery £20 towards his bill and to proceed to the appointment of a Master and Mistress at the following meeting. Accordingly on May 26th 1724, John Symonds was appointed first Master of the school at a salary of £15 per year, payable half yearly, together with meat, drink and washing and lodging. It was the 9th of June however, before Mrs. Mary Jennens was appointed Mistress at £8 per year.

The preparations were now almost complete. The brick school buildings were ready to be brought into use; the first intake of pupils had been nominated by the subscribers, their clothes ordered and a Master and Mistress appointed. So at the end of June the Order Book recorded that:

> "The 20 boys already belonging to the school and 10 girls shall from the opening thereof be clothed, fed and taught and also that a further 10 boys and 10 girls be clothed and taught only."

The expenses involved must have absorbed already most of the money that had been collected and subscribed. As well as the

£500 given by Riland Vaughton in 1722, £300 had been presented in 1724 by Mrs. Felicia Jennens (probably a relative of the Mistress), towards the cost of the building work. Each of the subscribers, and there were about thirty at this time, contributed a guinea or more each year. These sums would not however have been adequate to cover all the costs incurred.

One important item remained to be dealt with — the catering side — and this was attended to at the meeting of August 4th, at which Thomas Duncombe and Nehemiah Tonkes were ordered to:

"Provide the provisions for the Charity School for the next month beginning on Thursday next according to the directions underwritten.

Next Sunday all the children belonging to the Charity School are to have the dinner, but from and after only thirty boys and girls according as they are specified in this book.

First Sunday	: thirty pound of mutton 6 of roots or cabbage
Second Sunday	: eighteen pound of beef 6 roots or cabbage
Munday	: milk, poage* and dumpling
Tuesday	: fifteen pound of mutton 6 roots or cabbage
Wednesday	: pease porage* and 4 pound of bacon
Thursday	: fifteen pound of mutton 6 roots
Fryday	: hasly* pudding
Saturday	: Dumplings or Firmity*".

No mention is made of the cooking arrangements.

---

* See Glossary (Appendix G.)

Publick Education, particularly in the
CHARITY-SCHOOLS.

A

S E R M O N

Preach'd at

St. *Philip*'s Church in BIRMINGHAM,

Auguſt 9, 1724.

At the Opening of a

CHARITY-SCHOOL,

Built to receive an Hundred Children;

WHICH

Are there not only to be taught and cloath'd,
but alſo fed and lodg'd : With Accommoda-
tions for a Maſter and Miſtreſs.

By *THO. BISSE*, D. D.

Publiſhed at the Requeſt of the Truſtees.

L O N D O N:
Printed for W. and J. INNYS at the Weſt End
of St. *Paul*'s. 1725.

Title page of the 1724 sermon.

4

The School Opens
Early Years to 1750

The buildings were about to open their doors to the first intake. The structure, which had a frontage of 72 feet to the East, was elementary and incomplete and many problems would have to be faced, but the school came to life on Sunday August 9th 1724 when the thirty two boys (not thirty as recorded earlier) of whom ten were being taught and clothed only, and the twenty girls, ten of whom were taught and clothed only, were admitted and became the first Blue Coats. These children had been chosen by the subscribers, without any of the formalities that later became necessary. It was many years before the parents of incoming children were required to sign an agreement to abide by the rules of admission, for there were as yet few rules and the difficulties that were to appear in the future, of selecting a few from so many deserving cases, had not beset this first intake.

A sermon was preached that day at St. Philip's by the Reverend T. Bisse, entitled 'Public Education, particularly in the Charity Schools'. It is a very long address which was later printed and covers 40 plus pages — ample testimony to the stamina and endurance of the preacher and his congregation. The townspeople may have caught their first glimpse of the blue coats worn by the boys, soon to be a familiar sight to the citizens of Birmingham.

It was not long before more benefactors appeared to give financial assistance to this worthy cause. In the year of its opening, the school received a donation of £50 from Mr. William Norton, and Mrs. Elizabeth White of Whittington, near Lichfield, bequeathed to the Trustees for the use of the school, after the death of her sister, twenty five acres in Aston, known as Brook House Fields and Slow's Moor. This estate came into the possession of the school in September 1747. By the will of Benjamin Salusbury in 1726, a sum of 15 shillings a year was payable to each of the Rectors of St. Martin's and St. Philip's for a sermon to be preached each year in their own churches, for the benefit of the Charity School. This arrangement was to last for 200 years and be of great assistance to the school's finances. Then in 1727, Mr. John Harrison bequeathed £462. 12s. 2d. together with the remainder of a lease of land for fourteen years. These bequests and dona-tions, coming so soon after the opening of the school, indicate the recognition by the townspeople of the value of the school to the community. They also arrived opportunely to help to meet the heavy expenses incurred.

How the new institution consolidated and developed from this point is best described by the official records in the Minute Books. For the most part these entries require no explanation, just a little imagination and some willingness to step back in time.

1724   September 5th:
Thomas Duncombe of the Swan took the first apprentice to be sent out from the school. (Only one month from the opening date). Great care was taken in the placing of scholars as apprentices. The school aimed to produce literate, disciplined children and the committee expected any employer to recognise these assets and to treat them well. In several instances the committee took employers to task in positive fashion, when it was known that they were not fulfilling their obligations.

1725   January 12th:
"Ordered and agreed to pay Mr. Thos. Nicholson the Brewer the full of his bill being three pound one shilling and sixpence."

The drinking of ale at meals was a practice common to staff and pupils, who were allowed a daily ration. In view of the pollution of most of the water supplies by garbage and other offensive matter, it was as well that what was drunk had been through the brewery.

"It is also further ordered and agreed that Mr. Duncombe do send to London for three dozen of bibles, the like number of Common prayer books, one dozen of Dycher's spelling books with a dozen pair of blank indentures for binding of the Charity Children apprentices."

May 4th:
"Mr. Groves was to be paid £2. 13s. 0d. for teaching the boys and girls to sing Psalms to this time."

August 3rd:
First mention of the Charity Box which was hung on the wall at the entrance to the school. The box is now in the entrance hall of the administration building.

October 5th:
Stephen Russell, recently placed as an apprentice to a toy-maker, "shall have given him by the Society a new hatt, coat, waistcoat and breeches".

December 7th:
This decision was confirmed in an entry written by Thos. Duncombe. Hose and shoes were added to the previous list of items, "Also a Whole Duty of Man, besides the Bookes he learn'd at the Charity School (viz.) a Bible, Common Prayer Booke and Lewises Catechism and every boy that shall be put to apprentice from the Charity School shall have the like".

An entry during this year illustrates the difficulty of identifying the various names. The first two signatures for August 17th are both Richard Banner. The handwriting is remarkably similar, but the first belongs to Dr. Banner and the second is that of Richard Banner, Ironmonger, probably a family relation. There was a boy in the school named Robert Banner and one named John Vaughton.

1726   March 29th:
"Six ashen chairs and an oaken table made Oval large and to hold a dozen people for furniture of the Master's Parlour and three more chairs of the like sort for the use of the Mistress's school to be ordered and bought by Mr. Duncombe."

July 5th:
"Whereas Mr. Thomas Ashwell has offer'd to bake the bread for the Charity School gratis and Mr. William Cooper has offer'd to grind any or all the corn that shall be used in the Charity School toll free, therefore it is thought proper by the subscribers here present that corn shall be bought and ground and baked as aforesaid and the paste to be made at the school."

Mr. Ashwell was a prominent subscriber.

1727   February 24th:
Mr. John Cooper replaced Mr. Symonds as Master at £12 a year.

1728   February 5th:
Some concern about the legal status of the school was expressed and it was decided:

"That five guineas be paid to Mr. Stuart to be given to the Attorney General for his opinion and direction about the said school".

March 29th:

Among the twelve governors elected for the coming year were Richard Banner, John Banner and Samuel Banner.

April 16th:

Mr. Stuart was asked to obtain a decree for establishing the school without loss of time.

April 30th:

For the services attended in St. Philip's:

"The Charity boys shall sit on the North side in the Organ Gallery in the seats appointed for that purpose and the girls to sit on the South side thereof according to the general custome in other Charity schools".

1731 March 16th:

"It is ordered that a decent monument of stone be erected in memory of Mr. John Harrison, late of Erdington, a great benefactor to the Charity School."

At the same date it was decided to order a chest with three different locks and keys for holding documents relating to the school. This same chest remains in the Secretary's office, more than 250 years on.

June 1st:

Mr. Tonkes was asked to view an estate at Spark Brook, of about 39 acres. Eventually this was bought for £680.

The rents and profits were to be applied for ever to the maintenance and education of Charity children. Land and property bequeathed or bought, as in this instance, provided the solid, conservative base for the school's future growth. The market value of these assets rose steeply at times and occasionally some asset or other could be sold at a handsome profit to realise the cash required for expansion. Holding these assets on the other hand, generated a steady, annual income from rents that was reliable and predictable.

June 29th:

The Mistress was allowed an assistant.

1732

Several meetings this year were held at the Castle Inn.

1733 May 22nd:

A boy was admitted:

"provided the Overseers (of the poor) pay two guineas as usual he being parish child."

1736 July 6th:
"No more children shall be admitted into the said school or recommended upon the list, till the circumstances of the school will admit of it and as it has been observed that the boys have taken greater liberties than heretofore it is agreed that the Reverend Mr. Vyse be desired to admonish the Master."

The Master was in fact dismissed.

October 5th:
John Cottrell appointed Master. This was to be a splendid appointment. After many years as Master, he became a highly respected member of the Committee. He died in 1792 and was probably the son of the John Cottrell who signed the 1722 land lease.

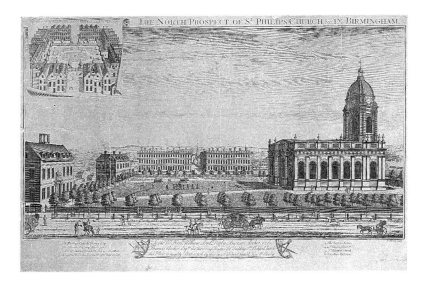

Wm. Westley's North Prospect of St. Philip's Church, 1731.

1. The school building shown in this print corresponds exactly with the print of the school on the front cover, taken from W. Hutton's *History of Birmingham*, 1819.

2. The note written by Westley on the lower left of the inscription reads "A New Charity School wherein are Cloathed Taught and Maintain'd upwards of 80 Boys and Girls.

1740   May 13th:
> "It is also further agreed that Mr. Thomas Turner shall take care to buy a cow for the use of the said school."

1741   March 10th:
> It was agreed to accept children from Fentham's Charity at a rate of £4. 5s. 0d. per annum.

In the year 1690 Mr. George Fentham, a successful Birmingham mercer, bequeathed a large property for the purpose of creating several funds for the benefit of the poor of Birmingham and Hampton-in-Arden. He directed that a portion of his estate should be divided into two equal parts, the yearly rents of one part to be employed for the relief, maintenance and other benefits of such poor inhabitants of the Parish of Birmingham as should be deemed worthy of it by the ratepaying inhabitants of the town, of full age, residing within the space of 200 yards "from and about the Bull Ring". He also directed that a further annual sum of £10 should be spent for the purpose of "teaching to know their letters, spell, and read English" poor children, either male or female, of necessitous parents. These children were clothed by Fentham's Charity in a green coat to distinguish them from the blue coats.

1742   July 13th:
> "The rest of the creditors of the said school shall be paid the sum of four shillings in the pound in proportion to their debts."

1743   March 29th:
> The school was able, after a gap of seven years, to admit thirteen more children.

1744   December 25th:
> £220 to be taken from the chest and invested in a Government security.

These extracts bring us to the end of the first Order Book, covering the first twenty or so years of the school's existence. The Order Book is a business record, sometimes annoyingly terse and vague when read at this distance in time. For instance there is no clue as to the precise nature of the financial crisis that caused the annual intake of children to be suspended in 1736 and not resumed until 1743. Nor are we told why in 1742 creditors were paid one fifth of their bills but in 1743 it was possible to take money from the chest for investment.

The Order Book is written in dispassionate, objective language, setting down facts and decisions without sentiment or sentimentality or, indeed, comment. We are fortunate, however, that the Book exists at all. There can surely be few documents of its age, relating to early eighteenth century Birmingham society, that survive and are in safe keeping. This is equally the case with the subsequent records that take us through to the twentieth century. We do learn however, that Sam, Richard, and John Banner had died, as had Nehemiah Tonkes and Henry Carver. The Reverend Mr. Vyse had replaced William Higgs as the Rector of St. Philip's. In 1744 the annual subscriptions had reached the total of £128. 18s. 0d. In that year too, Sam Banner had left the school a £100 legacy and a legacy of the same amount was received from M. Bakewell. The sermons at the two churches had brought in £83. 19s. 1¾d. Those of the original trustees and subscribers who remained could see that their concept of a charity school was well established and that their work, money and goodwill had brought the school to a favourable position.

5

The Second Half of the Eighteenth Century

1750 December 18th:
"That Isaac Westler shall be allowed the old shoes as an advancement of the price for mending the same until there be a reduction in the price of leather which is now at 10*d* or 10¼d by the hide."

1752 January 14th:
Mrs. Jennens who had been Mistress since the opening of the school resigned on account of age and infirmity.

April 7th:
Resolved that no child under the age of seven should be admitted in any circumstances.

There follows a long sequence of entries showing the election each month of four joint Treasurers and Managers. This cumbersome arrangement was continued for many years.

1758 November 21st:
"Agreed that every meeting after the Charity Sermons shall be at such Publick Houses as shall happen by rotation from this time forward."

1759 March 13th:
"It is further agreed that no Dissenting Child of any denomination whatsoever shall be admitted into the Charity School."

This harsh decision was probably a response to an approach from the Non-Conformists and led to the establishment in 1760 of the Non-Conformist School in Graham Street, New Hall Hill.

June 5th:
The Committee deprecated the action of a subscriber who sold for three guineas his right to nominate a child into the school and expelled him from the Society.

1760 September 23rd:
A boy was expelled:

"for the insult and abuse the Master of the said School has suffered from the said boy's Mother".

September 30th:
"No child after they are admitted into the Charity School shall be suffered to speak to their parents or next friends, nor receive any money, victuals or other indulgence bar on such Holy Days as are appointed for them to go out, that is to say a week at Christmas, Shrove Tuesday, Mid Lent Sunday, four days at Easter, four days at Whitsuntide, two

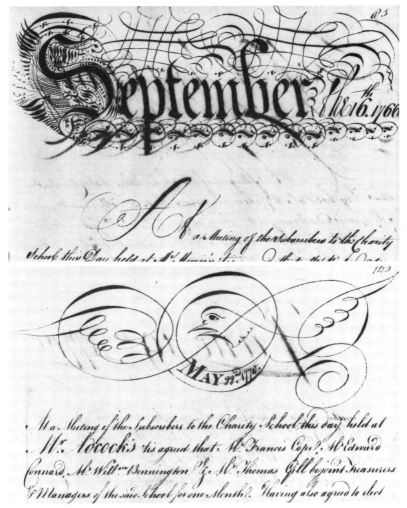

Fine and imaginative penmanship in the Order Book entries of September 16th 1766 and May 22nd 1770. Penmanship of this quality was the exception rather than the rule.

days at Michaelmas and every one to be at the school precisely at the time fixed by the Master every night upon pain of being confined at home the next Holy Day. . . . And that the Children be not suffered to take candles to bed . . . and that if any two or more of the children shall at any time form any pernicious scheme, conspiracy or combination the first that is concerned therein shall be imprison'd for one week and at the end thereof shall be severely whipt, stript and expelled from the school."

The uncompromising harshness of this order has to be considered in the context of the times, when lawlessness was a feature of the streets and over 200 crimes were capital offences. There is no doubt either, as the following entry shows, that in these years the school contained a number of boys who were causing considerable trouble, and that a warning of severe measures against indiscipline was necessary.

1761 March 24th:
Eight boys:

"have been guilty of many enormous crimes and misdemeanours. It is therefore agreed that they shall all be expelled . . . but if any Masters will take any of the said boys they shall have the same allowance as usual".

1763 October 25th:
John Cottrell resigned as Master. Samuel Whitehouse replaced him in January 1764 but proved to be unsatisfactory and he was succeeded by Ambrose Hill in May 1765. John Cottrell now became a member of the Committee after 27 years as Master.

1766 January 7th:
"An Ensurance be made for the School goods and Brewhouse to the amount of £500."

September 16th:
"George Craven be put apprentice to Matthew Boulton for seven years to learn all his arts."

Boulton, the renowned industrial pioneer, was a subscriber to the school and in 1767 was one of the four Treasurers. His works at Soho produced a wide variety of metal goods from buttons and coins to spurs and swords. Approximately 700 men were employed in the factories. When he and James Watt, the Scottish engineer, became partners, the Soho works converted from water to steam power and manufactured a range of engines for factories in the U.K. and abroad. Together with a number of distinguished, local men he instituted the Lunar Society. Meetings of the society were held at full moon each month, initially at Boulton's home on Handsworth Heath. The membership included James Watt, Erasmus Darwin, Dr. Priestley, Josiah Wedgwood and John Baskerville the printer.

1768 August 16th:
New Master to be advertised for. Candidates were instructed to:

"send or bring their specimens of writing and letters of recommendation".

September 20th:
Thomas Chaddocke made Master at £25 a year.

1769 September 12th
"It is also agreed that Mr. Saml. Grubb do compleat the two statues of a boy and girl which is to be erected over the door of the Charity School."

These two stone figures are now kept inside and those under the clock tower are replicas. Underneath the figures are the words:

"Train up a child in the way he should go and when he is old he will not depart from it."

"We cannot recompense you, but ye shall be recompensed at the resurrection of the just."

The figures show strikingly the dress of the children. (*See page 73.*)

1770 March 20th:
James Meer replaced Thos. Chaddocke as Master.

1771 January 1st:
"It is also agreed that Mr. Grubb shall have all the money that is collected towards erecting the statues over and above the thirty guineas he has already received."

1772 April 28th:
"It is agreed that Samuel Pardoe, who is afflicted with a scrofulous distemper shall be sent at the expense of this Charity to some seaport town for to receive the benefit of the salt water."

November 3rd:
James Meer resigned and Samuel Haye was appointed Master. There had now been five Masters in the nine year period 1763 – 1772. As the Order Book has nothing to say on this matter we have to guess the reasons for this rapid turnover.

A gap now occurs in the records as the volume (or volumes) covering the years 1773 – 1781 is missing. Whatever happened during these years must have called for an energetic approach in order to put things right, for the committee appointed in 1781 showed great concern about documents and leases, and a highly efficient system of administration began. The first entries show that Mr. Haye had been succeeded as Master by a Mr. Kempson who now in turn sent in his resignation. In fact the school was without a Master for some months until finally Mr. Ireland was appointed.

1782   January 15th:
A complaint was laid before the Committee of an apprentice from the school having been ill treated by his employer.

"It was resolved to apply to a magistrate for a warrant for Mr. Bayliss".

The latter quickly promised to mend his ways and the charge was dropped.

March 26th:
Plans for enlarging the school premises were considered and accepted. In the 1724 – 1784 copy of *Historical Account of the Blue Coat School*, this expansion is mentioned as well as a previous one during the year 1777:

"In the year 1777 the school was enlarged by building a schoolroom on a part of the back court and a lodging room over it: but the school room being found too small, that and the lodging room, were in the year 1782, extended over the whole court."

April 23rd:
"Resolved that the keeping of pigs at the school be discontinued as the profits thereof appear to be inadequate to the inconveniences arising therefrom."

1783   June 2nd:
"Resolved that each child's stockings be shifted as often as possible with convenience, once in a month at farthest."

September 8th:
The Committee needlessly and rather high handedly provoked a dispute with the Reverend Charles Curtis, Rector of St. Martin's. A letter from him was received on this date:

Parsonage, Birmingham

The illiberal behaviour of the Committee for the Charity School in not acquainting me with the gentleman appointed to preach the sermon at St. Martin's, puts me under the necessity of informing you, their Chairman, I shall not give up my pulpit unless that respect is paid me which I think due as Rector of this Parish.

Charles Curtis

This dispute became more intense when Mr. Curtis refused to lend his pulpit on denominational grounds to the clergyman selected by the Committee. Eventually the dispute was referred to the Bishop of Coventry, the Rector himself preached the sermon and honour was saved all round.

1784   February 23rd:
"Resolved that 1,200 books be printed, containing the rules of the school with a list of the subscribers thereto and an abstract of the receipts and payments for the year 1783 and also a short account of the school from its institution."

This is the booklet *Historical Account of the Blue Coat Charity School, Birmingham 1724 – 1784.*

September 6th:
Three boys:

"having, without leave, left the school on Monday the 30th past, gone to Stone Bridge in the road to Coventry and did not return 'till the next day. For which offence the Master had flogged them: but the crime appearing to this committee of a very heinous nature . . . Resolved that they flog each other in the presence of the Master and that they be confined at the school the Michaelmas holidays".

1785   March 8th:
Mr. Line was appointed Master, Mr. Ireland having been required to resign.

1787   November 12th:
A building in Bull Lane was offered to the school for £300.

"Also all those three messuages or tenements formerly 5 messuages or tenements with the apprts thrin descrd to be situated togr in Bull Lane . . . were granted bargained and sold to sd. Charles Curtis, Spencer Madan, Joseph Gibbs, Philip Hammersley, Robert Wheeler, John Bird, Thos. Beilby, James Osborne and Peter Kempson . . . subject to the payt of sd ppal sum of £250 & int to sd Wm. Eaves".

This extract from the land titles gives us the names of nine of the trustees in this year. Charles Curtis was, as we have seen,

Rector of St. Martin's; Spencer Madan was the Rector of St. Philip's.

1788   January 21st:
It was decided that in future all children were to be inoculated against smallpox before being admitted.

1789   May 25th:
An area of land behind the Bull Lane houses (acquired in 1787) was bought for £100.

1791   October 17th:
A meeting was thought to be needed to:

"fix upon what additional buildings will be necessary to be made".

The recent purchases of land and buildings in and around Bull Lane were essential and preliminary moves to allow the school premises to be further enlarged and improved, as indeed they were in 1794, providing extra accommodation and playground areas.

1792   December 31st:
Newspapers announced the death of John Cottrell —

"so good a man and liberal a benefactor".

1793   November 11th:
The girls were

"to assist in making the flannel waistcoats intended for the army in Flanders".

There are not many references to the world outside the school. This one reminds us that the French Revolution and the Napoleonic Wars were absorbing the attention of all of Europe and of the British Government.

November 18th:
£700 – £800 to be borrowed from the Taylor and Lloyd Bank for the new buildings.

1795   May 4th:
Four acres of land on Birmingham Heath (for use as a garden) were to be leased for 999 years at a yearly rent of one shilling from the Lords of the Manor of Birmingham — the Earl of Plymouth, Christopher Musgrove, Henry Howard and Edward Bolton Clive.

Matthew Boulton, Joseph Gibbs and John Ward had been appointed to look into the management of the school and seem to have been instrumental in securing this concession which, by 1828, was producing a rental income of £96. 10s. 0d.

There is now the second break in the records, none being available for the years 1796 – 1801. From the opening of the school to December 1783, a period of sixty years less a few months, a total of 500 boys and 211 girls had been admitted. For just over 70 years the school had been a focus of interest to the townspeople and the building was now a well known and respected landmark. With the additions of 1794 its appearance had altered and conveyed confidence in its future. In his *History of Birmingham*, first published in 1787 and revised in 1819, Hutton had lavished praise on the Charity School.

"It is a plain, airy and useful building, ornamented over the door with the figures of a boy and a girl in the uniform of the school, executed with a degree of elegance that a Roman statuary would not have blushed to own. . . . This artificial family in 1782 consisted of about ninety scholars of both sexes over whom preside a governor and governess both unmarried . . . Great decorum is preserved in this little society . . . This monument of a generous people was elevated to its present magnitude in 1794, at the expense of £2,500."

Legacies and bequests during these years (1750 – 1800) had greatly contributed to the strong financial position of the school. John Cottrell had donated £100 in 1789. In 1790 there was a legacy of £50 from an improbable sounding Louis Placide le Pileur and in the same year Elizabeth Hollier had bequeathed £200 and Joanna Harris £1,000. Both of the last named were of the Vaughton family. By Act of Parliament in 1798 for the enclosure of Birmingham Heath, a piece of land on that heath, about four acres in area and adjoining the little Hockley Pool, was vested in fee in trustees for the benefit of the Charity. In 1799 by the will of Mrs. Elizabeth Woolley, the school acquired a moiety* of an estate of seven acres of land in Garrison Lane, Bordesley. (The other moiety of this estate was bought in 1804 by the Committee). Also in 1799 Joseph Gibbs, William Brown and Henry Kempson "being persuaded of the great utility and very humane institution of The Blue Coat Charity School" bequeathed two messuages in Moor Street with the slaughter

---

*   See Glossary (Appendix G)

houses and premises attached and a piece of land about seven acres in area in the parish of Aston called Brickkiln Piece.

So the beginning of the nineteenth century could be welcomed with few if any reservations. The school buildings were sound structures, the finances were in good order and the management was efficient. The turmoil of the Napoleonic wars, that were to continue for another fifteen years, had little apparent effect on the school as it went about its daily routine.

Stone tablet which was removed from the Colmore Row building and is now in safe keeping at the school. Eventually it will be displayed.

6

The Revd. H Downing's Maid

This curious story, related in the records over a period of eighteen months, has been taken out for separate notice and for the sake of continuity. The affair began on September 5th 1782.

On this date Elizabeth Fieldhouse, apprentice to the Reverend H Downing of Harborough Hall, near Hagley, came to the Committee to complain of being ill treated by her employer and by his wife, particularly the latter. The Committee chose one of their members to investigate the complaint. At the following week's meeting, he reported "that he waited upon Mr. Downing the 11th instant and has great reason to think that the girl's complaints are well founded".

Convinced now that they had good cause to intervene on behalf of a former pupil, the Committee directed that the girl should be escorted back to her employer by Mrs. Fieldhouse (the girl's stepmother) who would deliver at the same time the written reprimand below.

16th Sept. 1782

Revd Sir,

We have sent your apprentice back again, and, upon deliberate and strict enquiry, are all convinced that she has been used very ill by you and Mrs. Downing: you say that she can neither brew nor bake, which is entirely your fault by not having her instructed in that business, as brewing and baking are not part of the education of our Charity School: you also say she is very dirty and lousy, which is not to be wondered at, so long as her dress is so mean and paltry, and she has been without a shift to her back for a month together, greatly to your disgrace. We therefore expect that in future you dress her in a decent manner, as a servant ought to be; to take care of her morals and send her to Church every Sunday; to treat her with tenderness and humanity (not to beat her) and let her have a good bed to lie on: then we make no doubt but she will behave as well as other servants in general do, if not better. We make no doubt but the girl has her faults and we have given her a strict charge to behave well to you both and

family, which she promises to do, provided she is treated
with propriety and not with cruelty as she has been; but if
you should continue to use her in the manner you lately
have done, we then shall be obliged to take such a method
as will be very disagreeable to you as well as to

Your hble Servants   Thos. Hurd Chairman
Edwd. Winfield
Peter Barnet
Edwd. Thomason
Wm. Simpson

This letter illustrates splendidly the mettle of the Committee
when presented with a case of alleged mistreatment of a former
pupil. The Reverend Downing was not easily cowed however, (or
perhaps it was Mrs. Downing) for he returned the following letter
by hand of Mrs. Fieldhouse.

Harborough 22 Sept. 1782

Gentlemen,

The apprentice which you have this day returned after much
wise consultation, shall be used according to her deserts. I
will take care and provide a proper place for her, if her future
conduct is not much better than the past.

I am with due respect
Yr. hble Servant
H. Downing

Mr. Downing's reply, together with Mrs. Fieldhouse's account
of her reception, spurred the Committee to the further action of
asking Mr. Winfield to make enquiries, but there is no record of
his efforts and the matter rested there until December 12th. On
this date, Elizabeth Fieldhouse attended the meeting to allege
"further ill treatment from her Master and Mistress and that her
Mistress yesterday ordered her to come to Birmingham". At this
the Committee "resolved that application be made to proper
Magistrates to summons the parties before them to determine the
matter". At some time between September and December Mr.
Downing had moved from Harborough Hall to Kinver and it was
from there that he sent this letter to the school:

Kinver Dec 18th 1782

Sir,

Elizth. Fieldhouse my apprentice eloped from her service
on Wednesday last, without the shadow of an excuse to

justify such conduct. I have therefore to request that you will acquaint the Governors that I think it is incumbent on them to compel her to return immediately to her place. If she does not return in a few days, I shall advertize her, and any person whatever that shall harbour or employ her, shall be prosecuted with the utmost vigour of the law.

I am Your's

H. Downing

Both parties were now threatening legal action. Rather surprisingly, the Committee decided to make a gesture of reconciliation.

"From the contents of the preceding letter and the opinion of Joseph Carless Esq. thereupon it was thought most prudent to decline carrying the resolution of the 12th instant into execution and that Elizabeth Fieldhouse should be sent back to her Master. It is therefore resolved that Mr. Price and Mr. Hurd . . . do take Elizabeth Fieldhouse to her service on Monday next and that Mr. Ireland give Mr. Downing the following answer this evening.

20 Dec. 1782

Revd. Sir,

      I have laid your favour of the 18th instant before the Governors and am directed by them to inform you that Elizabeth Fieldhouse will be conveyed to you on Monday next by one of the Governors, when it is hoped you will be at home to receive them.

Yrs etc.

R. Ireland

So on December 23rd Elizabeth was escorted back once more and Mr. Price and Mr. Hurd reported that after talking with both parties they were hopeful that the situation would improve. This hope can not be said to have been realised, although eight months went by without further trouble being reported. Then, on the 19th of August 1783, Elizabeth came to Birmingham "in a very shabby dress and complained to this Committee that she had been ill treated by her master and mistress". At the same time a letter was produced from Mr. Downing.

Kinver Aug. 20th 1783

Sir,

      I should have sent to you this day, to acquaint you of the ill conduct and elopement of E. Fieldhouse but I could not readily procure a messenger on account of the harvest. I have however dispatched a person on purpose with the clothes she pulled off immediately before her departure (in order as I suppose to make you believe she has been very ill used) to convince you that she is a very wicked girl indeed. She is become very headstrong and ungovernable that we know not how to manage her, and so intolerably impudent as to tell her mistress in my hearing that she was a Lyar. If such insults are to go unpunished, farewell to all order and subordination. I beg she may meet with such a reception as may (if possible) convince her of her folly and wickedness.

I must beg your pardon for troubling you with this, but as you are acquainted with her former ill conduct, I thought it most proper to acquaint you of this matter as early as I could.

I am etc.

H. Downing

The letter was addressed to Mr. Thomas Hurd, the Chairman of the Committee. It was resolved "to procure a man and horse to convey Elizth. Fieldhouse to Mr. Downing to-morrow". The letter below was sent at the same time.

Birmingham 22nd Aug. 1783

Revd. Sir,

The Governors of the Charity School, though ever ready to listen to the well founded complaints, and to take proper steps to redress the real sufferings of the children to whom they are appointed Guardians, will never be found to countenance disobedience to those under whom they shall be placed, nor to connive at, nor encourage an unprovoked and unjustifiable desertion of their several duties and employments.

As a proof of this their disposition and because that there appears to them, on examination of circumstances, some foundation for complaint to the Governors on the score of improper treatment, yet as it does not seem to them to be an adequate cause for the girls wantonly and hastily quitting your service, they have directed her to return thither in the charge of the bearer of this letter immediately.

The conduct of the girl the Governors condemn as being exceedingly reprehensible, but they are no less concerned to find that the mode of correction has been unusual and improper. She complains of having received, for some offence committed on Tuesday last, a violent blow in the face which almost cut through her lip. This she may have somewhat aggravated, as on examination there did not remain marks of any great violence. But still Sir, we appeal to your own feelings whether this be a proper or humane species of punishment. We are inclined to think that, like other girls of her age, she is impertinent enough and may sometimes stand in need of reasonable correction. The instance you mention of her having called Mrs. Downing a Lyar was of such a nature as to call for immediate and severe chastisement: but we trust to your humanity that where offence is given punishment will be inflicted with moderation and discretion.

The girl complains also of being kept short in clothes and that she seldom or never attends the duties of the church. The number of your family may keep her frequently at home on Sundays but we hope that she will be permitted to go oftener than on enquiry it seems she has gone heretofore: it being the care of the Governors of this Charity to see that the moral and religious, as well as the social duties, are punctually observed. And on the score of clothing we trust to your humanity in this particular, since in a family so large as yours the labour cannot be very trifling, and if the girl industriously and cheerfully do the business assigned her, you will take care that she is properly and decently cloathed. We conceive this to be scarcely the case at present, it appearing that she has had for some time past only one pair of shoes, and those so bad as to be hardly fit to be worn. Other parts of her clothing we hope will not escape your notice.

The girl appears to us hearty and strong and capable of laborious service and we have given her such injunctions as we hope will induce her hereafter to do her business to your and Mrs. Downing's satisfaction: and we persuade ourselves that while she thus conducts herself with industry, sobriety, decency and respect, she will be treated by you and Mrs. Downing with tenderness and humanity.

By order of the Committee
Thomas Hurd, Chairman

This long, reasoned plea made no impression on the Reverend Downing, who immediately took his quill and penned an equally lengthy reply.

Kinver Aug. 22nd 1783

Sir,

Yours I have just now received containing particular complaints of E. Fieldhouse, to which you seem to lend an ear, as tho' well founded. I shall not now, for the same reason I did not in my last letter, attempt to lay before you the many, I could almost say, numberless instances of disobedience that we have put up with, because it would exceed the limits of a sheet of paper. But I shall only in answer to your letter explain to you the reasons why she received that blow upon the face which you mention: 'twas Sir, for giving Mrs. Downing the lie: an instance of provocation that would not (if she had met her deserts) have passed so lightly. However improper you may deem this act, I must confess it does not strike me in that light. I must take the liberty of asking you what sort of punishment is to be given to an obstinate, perverse girl (who, when I have sent for her has refused to come, who, when she has been ordered to do a thing, has refused to do it) since you express your dislike to the mode of punishing her which has hitherto been pursued. With respect to the article of going to church I must tell you that she has been commanded to go, time after time, and the neglect arises from herself, as there is scarcely a Sunday but what she has an opportunity of attending once in the day and if you offer to punish her, she will set up such a yell, as would alarm the whole neighbourhood. She has much of the Swine in her composition, it is most difficult to lead or drive her. There is another matter you mention, viz, her clothes: of which she has sufficient, 'till such times she will take better care of them: she will sleep hours rather than take a needle in hand to mend them, and, I promise that neither Mrs. Downing nor my children shall mend them for her to encourage her idleness:- her shoes are entirely owing to the same cause, she will neither turn them nor unbuckle them from the time she has them new 'till they are worn out.

When she deserves encouragement, you may assure yourself she shall have it in abundance: but if she perseveres in her bad courses, I must request of you and the rest of the Governors to consent to the cancelling of her indentures for she has already given both you and me more trouble than can well be imagined.

I am etc.
H. Downing

Little over one month later, on September 29th.

"The Reverend Mr. Downing of Kinver called on the Chairman and informed him that his apprentice Elizth. Fieldhouse continued to behave ill and wished that a letter of exhortation might be wrote to her. Resolved that Mr. Theodore Price do draw up such letter in order to be forwarded to her as soon as convenient."

There is no record of the letter of exhortation but its effectiveness was no more than temporary.

Kinver 28th January 1784

Sir,

I write to inform you that E. Fieldhouse eloped last Saturday, and to request that you will not give yourself the trouble to send her back to her place as she has been the author of confusion in my family for some time back, and as we have hired another servant in her place.

I am your hble servant
H. Downing

Elizabeth attended the Committee meeting of February 9th and

"made complaints of her master and mistress. She was accompanied by Mrs. Webster, who promised to take care of her for a week".

On February 16th

"Mrs. Webster and Elizth Fieldhouse attended, when Mrs. Webster said that Mrs. Luke Kempson would take Elizth. Fieldhouse on trial the next day".

On February 23rd

"Mrs. Webster reported that Elizth. Fieldhouse had been with Mrs. Kempson from Tuesday last and that she heard no complaint".

That is the last we hear of Elizabeth. This narrative of her trials has been given in full, because it contains so many points of interest. It would be foolish, at this distance in time and on the strength of these letters, to attempt to judge the rights and wrongs of the issues and persons involved. It is however, a matter of some relief that the children who left the Charity School could still rely on its Governors for help in times of need.

7

The School to its Centenary (1824)

Just before the records resumed in 1802, there was a short armistice in the Napoleonic war, which was celebrated throughout the country. An account of the rejoicing in Birmingham in *Aris's Gazette* of October 19th 1801, mentions the school.

"The illumination . . . on Monday evening was one of the most splendid and brilliant Birmingham ever witnessed. There was scarcely a house that did not exhibit some beautiful transparency or device. The Free School, Blue Coat School (lighted by a private subscription) and other public buildings particularly attracted notice; and the immense fire of loads of coal in front of the Canal Office, at the end of a wide street, where an ox was roasting, had a very good effect."

Not many weeks later, a curious incident in the history of the charity was recorded in Langford's *Century of Birmingham Life*.

"A musical performance was given this month, in the various churches and chapels, for the benefit of one of our best charities — the Blue Coat School. The Committee thus express their obligations and return their thanks:

Nov. 9th 1801

The Committee return their very grateful thanks to all the Vocal and Instrumental Performers who generously and successfully exerted their splendid talents at the different churches and chapels for the benefit of the Blue Coat Charity School. As Mr. Weston has requested them to be sparing of their Acknowledgements to him, they reluctantly comply with his request; but think it their indispensable duty to inform the Subscribers to this Charity that, in a very infirm state of health, he has devoted a great part of the last five months to the composing, transcribing, teaching, and arranging of that Mass of Music, which has met with such general Approbation; and that he has declined the Acceptance of any Remuneration for his Labour, or Reimbursement of the Expenses which he incurred."

Mr. Weston made the following reply:

November 16th 1801.

To the Committee of the Blue Coat Charity School.

Gentlemen,

Happy in the Consciousness of having, to the utmost of my Power, contributed to the Support of your benevolent Institution, I am almost equally happy in finding that you have complied with my earnest Request, since from your chastized Praise of myself, in last Monday's Paper, the Interested, the Envious, and the Malevolent, will feel less Inclination to gratify their unamiable Propensities, than when, in July last, you so overrated my humble Talents and so overpraised my feeble Service: for I think it a Christian's duty to avoid throwing Temptations and Stumbling Blocks in the Way of the 'weaker Brethren.'

Far be from me the vanity of attributing the unprecedented amount of the last Collections solely to my Exertions; the high reputation of the Clergymen who have so distinguished themselves, by their excellent Sermons, on the different Occasions, forbids such an absurd supposition. To my numerous Vocal and Instrumental Friends who so readily and generously exerted their various Talents, without Fee or Reward, and who even refused to be repaid their Expenses, I return most sincere Thanks, assuring them that neither Distance of Time nor Place shall ever obliterate their kindness from my Remembrance.

I have the honour to be,
Gentlemen, with perfect gratitude and respect,
Your devoted servant,
Joseph Weston.

The flowery phraseology of this reply, the liberal use of capitals and the elaborate sentences will seem unbelievable to the late twentieth century reader but at the beginning of the nineteenth century none of these features were unusual.

The committee records resume in October 1802, in the middle of one of Europe's great wars. Normally the records contain no indication of the social background and upheavals of the period in which they were written but one of the first entries in this book gives a glimpse of the impact of the Napoleonic wars and the need to train recruits.

1803   September 26th
"Application having been made by the Earl of Dartmouth . . . for the use of the Boys School Room during wet and bad

weather for drilling the Volunteers, it is resolved that at the present crisis the application be agreed to."

October 17th

Mr. B. Line, the Master, having resigned, the following advertisement was prepared for insertion in the Birmingham papers:

Birmingham Charity School.

Wanted at Christmas next a Master to the said School properly qualified to teach reading, writing and arithmetick, he must be an unmarried man and well recommended for his good moral character, he will be comfortably accommodated with board, washing and lodging and must superintend the orderly management of the house and will have suitable encouragement for his attention and assiduity.

In December Edward Jones was appointed for a probationary year.

1805   February 4th

Mr. Wm. Ward and Mr. Wm. Pitt presented to the Committee the sum of £51 raised by an association of former pupils of the School.

The association was called originally the "Grateful Society"; later it became known as the "True Blue Society" and continued to make welcome contributions to the school's finances.

June 10th

It was decided to ask Mr. Hollins to clean the figures over the entrance to the school and re-site them if necessary.

William Hollins (1754 – 1843) was an architect. He is less well known than his son Peter Hollins (1800 – 1886) who achieved a wide reputation as a sculptor and was responsible for restoring the tower front of St. Philip's and for the statuary of Alton Towers. There is a reference in Gunnis's *Dictionary of British Sculptors* to a facade group of figures, supposed to have been executed by P. Hollins for the Blue Coat School in 1833. It has not been possible however to find any other mention or trace of these figures by way of verification.

1806   January 27th:

Three boys ran away:

"at length were discovered on the road to Bristol, with an intention of going to sea. The man sent in pursuit of them has brought them back."

The two younger boys were 13 and 12 years old.

March 3rd:
"Resolved that seventeen hundred of the Rules of the School be printed by Mr. T. Chapman, agreeable to the specimen delivered at £27 for two thousand."

This issue was in effect a second edition of the 1724 – 1784 booklet.

September 29th:
"The collection at the churches after sermons by the Revd. Jethro Inwood amounted to £115. 15s. 3¼d. . . . It being thought proper to make an offer of a ten pound note to Mr. Inwood to defray his expenses, Mr. Holt is desired to do it in as delicate a manner as he can."

1807   October 12th:
"It appearing to this Committee that Mr. Johnson cannot at present supply the House with milk . . . and as Mr. Freer reports the result of his enquiry at another place we find the price to be much greater than was at first supposed viz. ninepence a gallon . . . and from the enquiry made by Mr. Freer he is of the opinion that genuine milk cannot be had at a less price, it is therefore for the present the opinion of the committee with one dissenting voice that a third cow should be had and an additional quantity of land about 2 acres obtained for their keep."

A few days later a cow and "calf at her heels" was bought for £17.

1808   February 1st:
"The gentlemen deputed to enquire into the state of the Female department of the school do report that they found Mrs. Billingsley in good health and spirits and apparently equal to the duties of her office with a proper assistant. That they found Mrs. Baxter very ill and as she is constantly under the disadvantage of deafness they see great reason to believe that she is not capable of giving Mrs. Billingsley sufficient assistance as a teacher. That Mrs. Baxter acknowledges and laments her own inability. That it seems to them adviseable that a more competent assistant, active, intelligent and not exceeding 40 years of age should be provided as soon as Mrs. Baxter can be properly disposed of."

1809   April 12th:
"Resolved that on account of the low state of the finances only 15 children be ballotted for, at the usual time on Easter Tuesday next."

The ballot consisted of drawing from the total of subscribers, a number of names corresponding to the number of children to be admitted. These subscribers could then nominate a child of their own choice. Rules had been formulated to prevent any one subscriber from being drawn more than once in a given period of years.

In order to help restore the school's finances, an investigation of the domestic economy was now started. Several entries are taken up with details of this concern.

July 21st:
"The article of malt has now been under consideration and like that of tea and sugar seems to be very expensive to the Institution . . . Resolved that Mr. Forrest be applied to by Mr. Cheshire to know on what terms he will supply the House with about 111 barrels of 36 gallons each of good beer and 4 barrels of ale, to be supplied in a regular way for 12 months."

We learn also that 56 lbs. (25 kilos) of moist sugar had been used for wine. Taken with the previous entry, it is clear that a generous consumption of drink was condoned! The Committee also learned with dismay that the milk from the cows was being skimmed twice of its cream for butter making and promptly ordered that the night milk only should be skimmed once for this purpose.

The quotation received for beer and ale makes interesting reading.

"Small at 10s. a barrel and best Table Beer at 20s. a barrel of 36 gallons. Ale best old 66s. Best Mild 64s. Fresh Ale 58s. Porter 56s. Brown Stout 64s."

September 1st:
The Master's salary was advanced to £45 a year.

1810   February 20th:
Audited accounts showed that the arrears, that is the sums of money owed by the school to traders and suppliers came to £873. This amount was £126 less than in the previous year. These accounts were published in several local newspapers including the *Commercial Herald.*

1811   May 23rd:
The buildings in Bull Lane were to be demolished and the cleared area used as a playground for the girls, being first enclosed by a nine feet high (2.75m) brick wall. A surplus piece

of land 43 × 33 feet (13m × 10m) was to be let for housebuilding. Finally two building plots were arranged, one in front of Monmouth Street and both were leased by Mr. Barrows.

December 9th:
Mr. McCready offered the Theatre Royal for a benefit night for the school.

1812 March 2nd:
Mr. Saml. Hammond vested £600 in the hands of Trustees to provide an annual income for maintaining two girls at the school. These girls were to be allowed a buff colour ribband to distinguish them.

1814 August 29th:
It was decided to sell the cows and to let the farm land at Hockley and Green Lane. Over the last three years the farm had operated at a loss of £350.

1815 April 24th:
A stricter economy was ordered in the victualling department.

"Instead of purchasing ale and beer the same be brewed at home under the direction of the master and that seven brewings of eight bushels of malt be allowed annually for the use of the family and 6lbs of hops to each brewing to make 66 gallons of ale each brewing with beer in proportion."

May 29th:
In order to allow the girls more time for their education it was decided that the boys should make their own beds and sweep and mop their bedrooms.

October 29th:
Mr. Edward Jones the Master resigned after being reprimanded.

1816 January 5th:
Mr. Henry Jones was appointed Master at £80 per annum.

March 18th:
Lined corduroy breeches to be adopted for the boys instead of leather as being "more comfortable and decent in appearance".

1817 December 19th:
The Reverend Johnson of the Central School, London paid a visit and expressed his delight with what he saw but urged that Mr. Jones be sent to London for a short time to perfect himself in

the National System. The Committee acted on this suggestion, paying all the Master's expenses.

1819   January 29th:
No child was to be admitted in future under the age of nine.

June 21st:
"Mr. Capper has applied for a boy, as an apprentice, to accompany him to and reside at Para in South America; and he has fixed upon John Slater, whose friends have been consulted and they, with the boy, are quite agreeable."

November 15th:
Mrs. Snell the Mistress was dismissed forthwith for conducting herself "with a degree of levity" towards an apprentice. Unfortunately we shall never know more than is stated in these few intriguing words of condemnation.

December 20th:
"This Committee have to record that another daring robbery (the second during the year) has been committed upon the Charity, the Kitchen having been entered through the small window (from which a pane of glass was first taken in order to open it) and four Bacon Hams stolen therefrom . . . A person however, John Walker, who proves to have been brought up in the school and was apprenticed to Thomas Sly, whip thong maker, now near 18 years of age, is in custody on suspicion and who was taken at six o'clock of the morning that the robbery was committed, with the Hams in his possession."

1820   January 28th:
The annual cost per child was declared as £13. 8s. 6d.

1821   January 15th:
"The report of Mr. Henry Jones the Master being about to alter his situation by a matrimonial connexion with the Mistress of this seminary; now confirmed by an interview with him upon the subject."

Mr. Jones was asked to continue as Master "so long as there is not any family".

1822   October 7th:
"The Committee of the Birmingham Gas Company having very handsomely offered to light a lamp at the front door of the Institution gratis, if this Committee will provide a proper lamp. Resolved that the Gas Co., be requested to fix a

handsome lamp for the purpose and charge this committee with the expense."

1823   July:
Estimates were sought for fronting the North end of the school buildings (i.e. the Colmore Row end) with stone to correspond with the facade. A tender for £700 was accepted.

1824   Centenary Year:
"This year being the Centenary of the Institution it is re-solved that the same be celebrated in a public manner. (On August 4th).

That the children attend divine service at the Church and afterwards be treated at the school with a dinner of roast beef and plumb pudding with peas, early potatoes and ale. That the children have a week's holiday commencing on Monday the 2nd of August.

That the Committee meet at half past nine in the morning and accompany the Children to Church.

That a public dinner be ordered at the Royal Hotel at 4 o'clock at which the Revd. C. Curtis has promised to preside. That a paragraph be inserted in next Thursdays paper and an advertisement on the following Thursday and Monday.

That the Clergy and all other friends to the Institution be respectfully requested in the advertisement to attend and unite in the procession to Church.

That application be made to the Church and Chapel War-dens for the use of the Town beadles and for the bells to be rung.

That a medal commemorative of the occasion be struck and metal ones be distributed to the children."

Over this first 100 years the school had clothed, educated and maintained no less than 1,700 children of Birmingham. This was a notable achievement. In spite of financial problems at various times, particularly between 1736 and 1742, the school had kept its independence, relying upon the generosity of the townspeople to provide by annual subscriptions, donations, bequests and the collections at the Charity Sermons in St. Philip's and St. Martin's, the not inconsiderable amounts of money needed to cover annual expenses and to provide a reserve of funds for future develop-ments. Annual running costs had now reached almost £3,000, made up as follows:

Provisions	£1400
Clothes	£ 500
Salaries and Wages	£ 200
Taxes, Sundries, Furniture & Repairs	£ 650

Towards this amount, the Charity Sermons raised, in 1824, £297. 6s. 8½d. and subscriptions brought in £960. 12s. 0d. The rents from the various estates provided an income of approximately £1,000 and the dividends on money invested £200. It was rare for the annual income to provide a surplus over expenditure; more usually there was a small deficit. Expenses such as estate developments or major improvements to the school buildings had to be covered from the capital reserves that had been patiently accumulated.

The government of the school had been assured by a succession of capable men, unsparing of their time and energy. The lean years served to emphasise the solid gains of other years, as extra accommodation was provided and the number of children for whom the school opened its doors rose steadily. From 1724 to 1783 a total of 711 pupils had been admitted, roughly twelve per year. From 1783 to 1805 the total of admissions was 518, roughly twenty-three per year. From 1805 to 1816 the number admitted was 281, approximately twenty-five per year. A breakdown of these totals shows that about two thirds of the number were boys and one third girls.

If the school had been a requirement in 1724, it was now a necessity. With the Industrial Revolution in full drive, large numbers of workmen had moved to this great manufacturing centre and the 1720 population of 20,000 had swollen to 110,000 and was still increasing at an unbelievable rate. For every child the Blue Coat School admitted, there were hundreds who could not enjoy its privileges. Many parents must have waited with anxiety for the outcome of the annual ballot to know whether one of their children would find a sponsor. Once the ballot had been made and all the nominations had been received and considered by the Committee, a parent or guardian of each of the children to be admitted was required to sign the Order Book, accepting the rules of the Institution. For many years the majority of those signing made a mark in the book, since they were unable to write.

8
1825 – 1843
Surviving a Scandal

1825   January 3rd:
The Revd. Benjamin Howell's request that a few children be admitted into the school under a fund known as St. David's Charity, was agreed to by the committee. The terms were to be the same as for the Fentham Trust entrants.

May 9th:
The Revd. Thomas Cook received a letter, part of which is quoted and constitutes an authentic testimonial to the school:

May 8th 1825

Revd. Sir,

Having had the pleasure of hearing you this morning at St. Paul's Chapel, pleading the cause of a charity that in my humble opinion stands as the brightest ornament to the inhabitants of Birmingham, and having heard you give notice that you should address the children this evening, I humbly take the liberty of informing you that many respectable tradesmen of this town were once inmates of that Institution and are now subscribers to the same, many that were also once inmates of the said Institution have formed themselves into a True Blue Society, for the purpose of mutually assisting each other but, more particularly, of contributing by an annual donation to the funds of that Charity which fostered them in their infant years, thereby showing their gratitude and respect for the many favours received and the benefits which they now experience from their early introduction into that School.

The letter was signed — "Late a Blue Coat Boy".

December 19th:
"The Chairman reported that a deed of conveyance of the Bull Lane Estate dated the 29th December 1787 had been saved from destruction by Mr. Beech, clerk to Mr. Whateley, formerly brought up in this Institution, who found such

deed in the custody of a parchment dealer, preparing to destroy it."

1826   October 2nd:
"Edward Thomason Esq. Medalist to his Majesty having very handsomely presented to this Committee the following medals viz.

His Majesty King George the Fourth
His late Majesty King George the Third
His Royal Highness the Duke of York
The Right Honorable William Pitt
Lord Viscount Nelson
His Grace the Duke of Wellington
Edward Outram D.D. late Rector of St. Philip's
Sir Walter Scott
Monitor's Medal to commemorate the foundation of the
    Schools for National Education.

the same were deposited by them this 2nd day of October 1826 under the first stone of the Church now erecting at Holloway Head and intended to be dedicated to St. Thomas the Apostle."

The fate of these interesting medals is a mystery. St. Thomas's Church was badly damaged during the 1939 – 1945 war by bombs. In 1955 when its tower was made safe and a garden of rest laid out on the site, the foundation stone was moved. A plaque from under this stone, which recorded the cost of building the Church, was recovered and set into the wall of the arbour. No mention can be found however, of the medals, which should have been removed at the same time as the plaque. There is a brass plaque in St. Philip's Cathedral recording the death of Edward Thomason.

1828   January 3rd:
Mrs. Jones the Master's wife, resigned her post as Matron

"in consequence of differences that have arisen between Mr. Jones and myself".

1829   April 6th:
A freehold area adjoining the school and fronting Bull Street, known as Hollow Tooth Yard was bought for £1,995. The area was purchased from Mr. James Allison with the intention that sick wards, a laundry and other conveniences separate from the main building should be built on it and to allow the playground to be enlarged.

June 29th:

"Mr. Thomas Hicks, Albion Hotel, presented one Pound to this Charity being the amount received from James Bullivant for furiously driving against Mr. Hicks in Stafford Street."

1831   January

The Preface to the *Historical Account of the Blue Coat Charity School, Birmingham (Edition 1724 – 1830)* begins with this statement:

"In presenting to the public the following account of the origin, progress and actual state of the Blue Coat Charity School in Birmingham, the friends of the institution have the greatest satisfaction and confidence in recommending it to the zealous patronage and support of every inhabitant of

The mystery of the missing medals

WHAT happened to a set of medals deposited under the foundation-stone of St. Thomas's Church, Holloway Head, Birmingham, when it was built in 1826? They were not found when the stone was moved in the reconstruction of the site in 1955.

The matter has become of immediate interest to Mr. J. D. Myhill, house master at the Bluecoat School, Edgbaston. He is compiling a history of the School, founded in Colmore Row in 1724. The School moved to Metchley Lane in 1930.

In the course of its earlier history it became the custom to present pupils with medals marking special occasions. Among them, for instance, was a Nelson medal, struck to commemorate Trafalgar.

School records show that in 1826 Sir Edward Thomason, a noted medallist of his day, gave the School a set of his medals.

St. Thomas's Church was then being built, and the School gave the medals for deposition under the foundation-stone.

St. Thomas's, was, of course, badly blitzed during the last war. When its tower was made safe and the garden of rest laid out, the foundation-stone was moved and a plaque recording its being laid was incorporated into the new scheme.

But there was no mention of any medals.

Mr. Myhill says he has consulted all the obvious authorities—the Public Works Department and the Reference Library among them—but can find no record of the medals.

What is the solution of the mystery?

" I am loth to let my history of the School go to press without mention of the medals," he said. He invites the help of anyone who can throw light on what happened.

The 'Medals Mystery'. An article which appeared in the Bimingham Mail of 16th August 1962. It brought no results!

the town, who is anxious to provide a suitable and useful education for the children of the poor, an asylum for them in those years which most require superintendance and protection, a careful discipline of their minds in a system of virtuous and obedient habits and daily instruction in the principles and duties of the religion of the Church of England. In each and every one of these most important particulars, the supporters of the Blue Coat School are not afraid to challenge comparison with any other establishment of the same kind in the kingdom."

1831   November 7th:
A letter was sent to Mr. Redfern at the Public Office.

Sir,

Please to deliver to the Blue Coat Charity School by bearer, forty half pints and seventy pints from the seizures of false measures made by

Your obdt. Servt.
Oliver Mason (High Bailiff)

The 110 confiscated cups were gratefully acknowledged.

1832   January 16th:
The True Blue Society forwarded a donation of £40.

December 24th:
Mr. Jones resigned. *Aris's Gazette* of January 14th 1833 announced that he had been appointed Master of Yardley Free Grammar School.

1833   February 18th:
Mr. Josiah Jacques was appointed to replace Mr. Jones at a salary of £100 per annum.

1835
The first mention in the records for this year that there was anything amiss was a statement of January 26th — four days before the Annual General Meeting.

"Thomas Paine having appropriated large sums of money belonging to this Charity to his own use in the manner stated in the report which renders him ineligible to serve on a Committee."

The report which had been prepared for the A.G.M. was presented on January 30th, and gave this account to the subscribers present.

"Your Committee have now the painful task of bringing under the notice of the subscribers a circumstance which has caused them much uneasiness and anxiety. In the month of September last the Committee was surprised to find that the Bank Account was much overdrawn and on enquiry they discovered that Mr. Thomas Paine (who has been for about fifteen years an active member of the Committee and is one of the Trustees of the Charity Estate and who as far back as the year 1820 was appointed one of the Inspectors of Accounts) had not paid over to the Treasurers various sums received by him for rents. On being called upon for an explanation, Mr. Paine in the month of October furnished a statement of the sums received by him and not paid over, amounting to £1,544. 19s. 8d. The Committee thought proper immediately to place the Books and Accounts of the Charity in the hands of Mr. William James, Accountant, for examination and the result of his investigation shewed that the statement delivered in by Mr. Paine was correct.

During the investigation of the Books and Accounts Mr. Paine, thro' the medium of the Chairman and other members of the Committee, repeatedly expressed his ability and determination to liquidate the amount due from him at an early period, and he did between the discovery of his defalcations and the 24th of November, pay three sums amounting to £265, leaving a balance of £1,279. 19s. 8d. but in the latter end of December, after the most urgent applications from the Committee, they had the mortification and disappointment to learn that Mr. Paine was insolvent.

The examination of the Accounts has led to the discovery that Mr. Paine has been in the habit of retaining monies of the Charity in his hands from time to time, during the past four or five years and the Committee can only account for the non discovery of these deficiencies by the fact that Mr. Paine (in whose integrity both the Committee and Auditors had the utmost confidence from his being so old and active an officer of the Institution) prepared the accounts and attended the Auditors at their examination of them and the Committee have no doubt that deception and misrepresentation was practised by him to cloak the transactions alluded to."

The report went on to state, optimistically, that arrangements were being negotiated in the hope of recovering some part of this heavy loss. These arrangements appear to have consisted of an offer by Mr. Paine, made through Mr. Whateley, to pay 3s. 4d. in the £, (i.e. one sixth of what he owed) and for an insurance in favour of the Charity, on Mr. Paine's life. Nothing is shown to have been recovered however. No doubt the members of the Committee would have preferred to limit public knowledge of this affair since it reflected a certain amount of discredit on the administrative system of the Charity and could have had an adverse effect on the financial support received. Their first move was to decide that in future the accounts should be audited half yearly by an independent accountant.

It was too much to hope for that there would be no outcry. On February 23rd there appeared a pamphlet, sixteen pages long, entitled: *Hole and Corner Work! An address to the people of Birmingham on the peculation at the Blue Coat School.* The pamphlet was written by J. Allday, a self styled opponent of injustice and malpractice, who was no newcomer to this kind of situation. He urged that a public inquiry should be held to uncover the true facts. Paine's fraud, he alleged, had been discovered in September 1834 when a banker asked a Committee member whether he was aware that the School account was much overdrawn.

In spite of this knowledge, continued Allday, Paine was allowed time to settle the debt and not denounced, as he should have been. As a result, his services were employed at a Music Festival in the Town Hall, on behalf of the General Hospital, in the following month. Allday stated categorically that he could produce many witnesses to prove that at this Festival, Paine had found seats in the gallery for people with tickets to the body of the Hall, charged them 10s. 6d. extra and put the money in his own pocket. The trustees were culpable also, he claimed, in not making public Paine's insolvency until February 1835, since this allowed him in the interval to impose on others who were not aware of his condition.

The difficulty, as Allday admitted, was that it appeared to be impossible to invoke the law in the case of a fraudulent Trustee. With this admission, his vehemence rose to new peaks.

"Men of Birmingham! can you repress your indignation? Will you look calmly on and permit such demonaical knavery to be committed with impunity? And the Trustees of the Blue Coat Charity School tell the subscribers to the Institution that there is no law by which they can compel this Thomas Paine to disgorge his ill gotten plunder or by which they can punish him? Gracious God! do I live in England where property is held sacred and where the petty thief who steals forty shillings is transported and the wholesale, reckless thief who robs the sacred funds of a Charitable Institution of which he is a Guardian, is not to be punished?"

At the end of the pamphlet, and more telling perhaps than all that preceded it, is this addition:

"Latest News P.S. Thomas Paine sent in his resignation this day as one of the Committee of the Association for the Prosecution of Felons."

The last we learn of this unfortunate affair is that in March, the Trustees were obliged to sell £1,100 of Government stock to cover the deficit at the bank. Very opportunely, the school received a legacy of £1,000 in May, from Fanny Tabberer of Tenby, Pembrokeshire.

September 28th:
Each child received a medal commemorating the tercentenary of the translation into English of the Bible.

1838   *April 30th:*
"The Committee having understood that cigars or tobacco have been smoked in the Assistant Teachers' Room, resolved that such a practice is very objectionable and must not be repeated within the building."

The battle for clean air seems to have started a long time ago!

June 25th:
It was decided to buy Coronation Medals (Queen Victoria) for presentation to the children, Master and Matron.

August 27th:
A report was presented, showing the cost per head of the children admitted during the last seven years. This amounted to £14. 17s. 1d. per annum, including clothes.

This calculation seemed to be capable of being adjusted to circumstances. When the treasurers of Fentham's Trust and St. David's Society, who were paying £11 per head to the school for their elected children, protested about the proposed increase, further calculations reduced the figure to £12. Even so, it was always a matter of surprise to outsiders that the school could be run so economically.

1840   *February 24th:*
Mr. Jacques resigned as Master.

April 9th:

Mr. William Wallis was appointed as Master.

October 14th:

"The Committee were called together specially in consequence of Mr. Wallis the Headmaster having early yesterday exhibited symptoms of mental derangement or at least a high state of excitement so as to render it necessary under the direction of Dr. Evans and Mr. James Wilkes to put him under restraint."

The post of Headmaster was promptly offered to Mr. James Foster, a former applicant.

1841   July 12th:

"This Committee are of opinion it would be a great benefit to the Birmingham Blue Coat Charity School if a physician and a surgeon would undertake gratuitously the regular visitation and care of the establishment."

An advertisement to this effect appeared in *Aris's Birmingham Gazette* and on September 20th Dr. Bell Fletcher was appointed Physician and Mr. William Tarleston surgeon.

New Street 22nd Sept. 1841.

Gentlemen,

I thank you for the very flattering manner you did me the honour of selecting me Surgeon to your highly valuable Institution. It shall always be my desire to make myself as useful as possible to the School and to retain your good opinion.

I beg to say that I shall be happy to supply all the medecines required for the school for a month or two (without any charge) until you make some arrangements with a Druggist.

I am Gentlemen
Your obedient Servt.
William Tarleston.

1843   The Special Committee Report

On the 31st January, at the Annual General Meeting, a resolution was passed

"that a Committee of 13 subscribers be appointed to investigate the condition and circumstances of the several Trusts and Property of the school, the system of education and the general management of the Institution".

The report of this body was presented on June 6th at a special General Meeting. It is a comprehensive, clear document, divided into three main sections.

a) Trusts and Property

A renewal of trustees was thought to be necessary or advisable in all cases, consequent upon deaths and removals. A new survey of the estates was recommended and the drawing of maps.

b) System of Education

A number of criticisms were offered:

"Because in no class, above half the lessons are heard by any master."
"That the hours afforded to the girls for teaching are much too few."
"Because the Master has no time wherein to inspect the detail of the several classes and make minute examination of the progress of each boy."
"That the Matron is unable from other occupations to take part in the education of the girls."
"That the girls are taught to write by the Junior male teacher, which we think objectionable."

These criticisms were followed by an appendix that provides a great deal of information on the internal organisation. There were six boys' classes, each averaging twenty, four girls' classes each averaging twelve. The daily routine for the boys was:

6.00	Rise, clean shoes, wash
7.30	Assemble in school room for prayers till 7.50
8.00 – 8.30	Breakfast
8.30 – 8.55	Play
9.00 – 12.00	School
12.00 – 1.00	Play
1.00 – 1.30	Lunch
1.30 – 1.55	Play
2.00 – 5.00	School
5.00 – 6.00	Play
6.00 – 7.00	Singing
7.00 – 7.30	Supper, followed by prayers
8.00	Bed

Wednesday and Saturday afternoons were holidays on one of which they were taken for a walk.

"There have been no means of exercise provided for them until the present week. We now have a gymnastic pole erected in the Boy's playground."

The girls' routine was patterned to the domestic requirements. They were employed in household work for several hours each day. Older girls were employed in the Laundry, others in mending, cleaning and waiting on tables. They were certainly taught less than the boys as a result.

The report disapproved of:

"the multifarious engagements of the Master, some of which are unsuitable to his position and some quite irreconcilable with each other and encroaching so much upon his time and attention as to render it quite impossible for him to discharge properly or efficiently the duties of either teacher or superintendent."

c) General Management

This section dealt with:

Diet — considered to be adequate
Clothing — the supply was thought to be too scanty.
Employment and Exercise — it was urged that the privilege of playing in an open field be obtained for the children.
House arrangements — better washing facilities were needed.
Duties of Master and Matron — the appointment of a Steward, to relieve them of many duties, was suggested.
General rules — several ideas were put forward concerning the selection of entrants.

The report was impressive and thorough. Most of the recommendations were accepted and were put into effect over the next few years, to the benefit of the school. By focusing attention on the school's estates, it led to a vastly improved and systematic approach to their management and a consequent increase in the revenue they provided. Lastly, the close investigation made of the trusts, many of which were in need of renewal or of legal action to consolidate them, led directly to the Act of Parliament, two years later, which resolved all these problems and allowed the school to fight off a threat to its independence, later in the century.

9

1844 – 1864

1844   March 5th:
   Counsel's opinion was received on the state of the Trusts. As a result, the Committee decided to apply to the Court of Chancery for approval of a scheme and then to Parliament for an Act to confirm the scheme. Some concern was felt about the possibility of the School's assets coming under the control of a dissenting body of subscribers and being diverted from their original purpose. (In this context, dissenter was anyone who was not a member of the Church of England and in particular a Protestant.)

   "In the present state of dissent in the town of Birmingham and the existence of a corporation of Anti-Church principles, an effort may at no distant day be successfully made by a body of subscribers (extended perhaps for that object) to change the principles upon which the school was founded . . . unless there always be Trustees of Church of England principles to interpose and keep a check on them."

1845   August 26th:
   "The Solicitor reports to the General Committee that the Act entitled 'An Act to vest the Estates and Property constituting the Trust Estate of the Blue Coat Charity School in Birmingham in the county of Warwick, in new Trustees, upon consolidated Trusts; and to provide for the management of the said Estates and Property, and for the good government of the said school and for other purposes' received the Royal Assent on the 8th instant and then became law and a print of the Act is now laid on the table."

   The full costs of securing this Act came to £1,200, a large sum it might be thought. It was without any doubt, however, a splendid investment. Agreements and understandings that had been satisfactory at the time they had been made, could possibly have been challenged at a later date and at the least led to unwanted litigation. The expenses involved in this exercise were met from the sale of Exchequer Bills and stock. At this time the school held about £3,700 stock in public funds and a sum of £6,950 in 3% annuities. Rents received from lands provided

£1,000 per year. In the year 1844 there were 212 children in the school.

1846   July 28th:
Among the book prizes awarded to those children who had been recommended by the examiners were:

> *Three weeks in Palestine: China: New Zealand: The Young Naturalist's Journey: Gleanings from Pious Authors: Nelson's Fasts and Festivals: History of Josiah.*

1847   April 5th:
The Estate Committee reported the sale to the Birmingham, Wolverhampton and Dudley Railway Company of land at Gibb Heath for £5,250, and the sale of houses in Wagstaff's Yard for £1,800 to the Birmingham and Oxford Junction Railway Company.

April 9th:
At the A.G.M. the school report praised the discipline of the pupils but thought their attainments too low.

"The period to which the children remain in the Charity extends to four years longer beyond the average time at which they leave our daily schools."

"With the sincere hope that this noble institution may continue to take the lead in the education of the working classes in this vast town.

Signed Wm. Gover M.A. Curate of St. Paul's
J.P.Hastings B.A. Curate of St. George's"

August 31st:
The Master, Mr. Foster, resigned to take over a private school at Bewdley. He was replaced in November by Mr. George Kirkland.

1848   June 27th:
"The honble. and Revd. Mr. Yorke reported the following case of theft.

On Thursday June 22nd 1848, Elizabeth —, aged 12 years 3 months, abstracted from Miss Slucock's drawers the sum of 2s. 6d. which she spent in sweetmeats. On Saturday 24th took a sovereign from the same drawer, 17s. of which has been recovered. . . . She changed the sovereign at a public house in Bartholomew Street . . . preferred changing it there as she thought at any other shop the parties would think the money was not her own."

The Revd. Yorke, Rector of St. Philip's for thirty years, later became the Dean of Worcester in 1875. The girl was expelled.

1849   January 30th
"The Master having also reported that Mrs. Sanders (the mother of John Sanders) and her daughter Mrs. Bailey and a man supposed to be the husband of the latter came to the school on the 26th January, between the hours of 6 and 7 o'clock a.m. (by agreement with the boys) and there sent in a quantity of bread and butter contrary to the Rules of the School; and that Mrs. Bailey had on several occasions come to the coal cellar window in Monmouth Street and given in various articles of food to her son."

November 27th:
"The following letter having been received from Mr. Cooper.

Birmingham 21st Nov. 1849

Dear Sir,

The Bearer Mrs. Bruff is the mother of Mary Ann Bruff who left the school the latter end of last March, in order to go to America with her father and mother. The Father worked for me fourteen years and was a steady Church going man but was induced to go to America hoping to do better there than in England. Unfortunately he was killed by the breaking of a mast before reaching America: his wife feeling very unhappy in a strange country, borrowed money to get back to England with her two children . . . I should be glad if the girl Mary Ann can again be allowed to return to the School. . . . John Bruff the father was brought up in the school."

The girl was re-admitted immediately.

1850   November 30th
Mr. Kirkland resigned.

1851   February 28th:
Mr. Edmund Hall of Queen's College, Cambridge was appointed Master.

September 19th:
Mr. Edmund Hall resigned!

November 3rd:
Mr. Robert Symonds was elected Headmaster.

1853   May 3rd:

A tender for £4,400 was accepted for the erection of additional school buildings. In the following year, 1854, the Annual Report described this work.

"The Committee advert with pleasure to the new erections — comprehending works of the highest utility and import- ance in an institution of this nature and magnitude. The improvements in the Wash house and Laundry and the culinary and other domestic departments will be found greatly to economise time and labour . . . the new plunging bath upon a larger scale, the enlarged School Room for the girls and the new suite of rooms, approached by a spacious stone staircase, distinct and separable from the other build- ings: the detached appartments for sick children appropriately fitted up under the superintendance of the Medical Officers — a new arrangement of offices and more extensive supply of water in every part of the establishment and the thorough drainage and ventilation of the school premises with increased playgrounds are some of the ad- vantages which will be apparent on an inspection of the new works."

November 29th:

The school received a donation of £500 from a former pupil who withheld his name.

1854   July 25th:

"An application having been made from the children to allow them a day's excursion into the country, resolved that it be allowed."

This outing became a regular annual feature and the tradition continued for many years.

1855   April 13th:

The School Examiners (local clergymen) suggested:

"That the Schoolroom should be supplied with parallel desks, that the several Classes be separated by means of curtains and low rods and that the arrangement should be so planned that each Monitor or pupil teacher should be under the immediate inspection of a Master, and the Junior Masters, pupil teachers and scholars should be all at the same time under the observation of the Head Master."

This suggestion was carried out in the Boys' School.

July 31st:
"Mr. Taylor of Moseley has offered the use of a field in his park for the children to spend a day there."

"The Revd. J.M.Aston presented to the Committee two photographic pictures of the children in the school."

"It appears to the Committee that the three general holidays at Easter, Midsummer and Christmas which afford 26 days are sufficient for the Master and for the Assistant Teachers in both departments — the Master having the privilege of leaving the school entirely in the Midsummer vacation."

One of the Revd. Aston's photographs taken in 1855.

1856   November 25th:
"The Finance Committee brought before this Committee the state of the finances. It appears that the debts owing amount to £2,016. 15s. 6d. including £1,479. 13s. 0d. due to the Bank. A letter was also received from Messrs. Attwood & Co. calling attention to the state of the account."

1857   April 17th:
"The first class of boys have in accordance with the suggestion of last year made a commencement of Euclid. They

appear to have been successfully instructed in the Defini-
tions and in the first twenty propositions of the First Book."

May 1st:
An application was received from the Royal Commission of the
Patriotic Fund, London, for places for boys on payment of £16 per
year. The Committee agreed to accept ten.

August 18th:
A resident House Steward was appointed.

September 29th:
The Headmaster resigned and a month later his post was taken
by Mr. Taylor.

1858   *January 26th:*
"The Revd. J.M.Aston reported that Emma Steele — 2nd
assistant in the Girls' School . . . had succeeded in obtaining a Queen's Scholarship of the First Class and he applied
for leave to be granted her to enter the Training College."

Emma Steele was a former pupil of the school.

March 10th:
At the request of the Committee the School was inspected by
one of Her Majesty's Inspectors of Schools. The Revd. Capel
carried out this first inspection (national as opposed to the local

The second of the Revd. Aston's school photographs.

system of inspection used up till this time) and became the regular inspector for the next twenty years. After his first visit he wrote:

"When I remember that a recent statistical enquiry has shown that the average age in Birmingham of the boys who leave school is almost identical with that at which your scholars are admitted, I cannot but fear that the ignorance of very many of the rising generation in this town must be very great."

"When I think what these children might have been, had they not been admitted, and what really useful members of society they will probably now become, I do trust that the funds of your Charity may never languish for want of aid."

May 11th:
"To consider the arrangements requisite to be made at the School on the occasion of her Majesty's visit to Birmingham. Resolved that platforms be erected in the Girls' Yard and on each side of the entrance in Monmouth Street".

"That the Committee subscribe £5 towards the expenses of the general scheme of decoration." (of Colmore Row)."

"That a Royal Standard be purchased for the occasion."

August 31st:
"Mr. Samuel Hasluck of Hazeloak House, Stratford, Essex this day met the Committee and presented the sum of one thousand pounds towards the funds of the institution, with a request that his name may on no account transpire beyond the members of the Committee and that it be noted as soon as possible on the Tablet in the Hall as follows:

Two brothers having been educated at the Blue Coat School Birmingham, one now deceased, the other having gained an independence by industry and perseverance, as an act of gratitude presented the sum of one thousand pounds, August 31st 1858 in aid of its funds, in addition to a former donation in the year 1853."

The former donation was that recorded on 29th November 1853, making a total of £1,500 received from these two ex-pupils. If evidence were needed even at this stage of the high value placed on the work of the school by the people of Birmingham, including of course its former pupils, it is easily found in this instance as well as in the contributions from the True Blue Society.

1859   January 25th:
Mr. Taylor resigned.

March 29th:
"That tinned iron plates and basins be substituted for
piggins* and trenchers* at present used by the children."

April 21st:
Mr. Welch was appointed Master.

April 29th:
The St. David's Charity was dissolved and no children spon-
sored by this fund were left in the school.

1860   April 13th:
A vigorous campaign had brought an increase in the annual
subscriptions from £667 in 1853 to £1,011 in 1859.

April 24th:
A Mr. Kindon wrote from London offering to give 20 beds with
bolsters and mattresses, so that the older boys could sleep singly
and not in pairs as had long been customary.

September 25th:
"It appears that several boys have suffered from bruises
arising from their playing at Hockey. Resolved for the future
this dangerous game be discontinued and football be substituted for it."

December 24th:
"Resolved that the House Committee be instructed to have
Capes, according to the pattern now submitted, made for
the whole of the boys in the school."

1862   March 25th:
"That the Headmaster be directed to prepare a register of
the books forming the childrens' library and that two pounds
be granted for the purchase of new books."

1863   February 24th:
"That the 18th day of March being the day appointed for the
marriage of His Royal Highness the Prince of Wales, the
same be celebrated by a holiday to the children of this school

---

*   See Glossary, Appendix G.

and that a medal commemorating the event be given to each child."

March 31st:
"That the cordial thanks of this Committee be sent to Messrs. Crowley & Co. for their kindness in conveying the children in wagons through the streets on the evening of the 10th inst., to witness the illuminations."

April 10th:
"A very desirable purchase has been effected of between 9 and 10 acres of land adjoining the estate of Sparkbrook. . . at a price of £2,000".

July 27th:
After 22 years as Honorary Surgeon, Mr. Tarleston resigned and was succeeded by Mr. Clayton.

10

1865 – 1890
A New School Site is Considered

1865   March 13th:
The Chairman of the Finance Committee was requested to attend a meeting of creditors of Messrs. Attwood & Spooner. By the following month it was clear that the school would lose £970 as a result of this bank's failure. On a balance of £2,200 only 11s. 3d. in the £ was paid.

The account was transferred to the Birmingham Banking Company but this bank also closed in 1866 and the account was again moved to the Birmingham Town and District Company.

   April 21st:
There were now 224 children in the school — 139 boys and thirty-five girls.

"In the early part of the year your committee directed their attention to the supply of water to the Institution, the average yearly cost of which since the Water Works Company has charged by meter having been £43. With the view to effect economy under this head and to diminish the consumption of soap in the wash houses, a plan for utilising the rain water has been carried out. An underground tank that will hold 20,000 gallons, has been constructed in which is collected the whole of the rain water from the roofs of the buildings; from thence it is pumped by steam power to a cistern at the top of the house to supply the washhouse, the boys' and girls' lavatories and other offices of the establishment.

An apparatus has also been laid down for warming the Schoolrooms and Dining room with steam pipes which has proved very effectual and added greatly to the comfort of the children during the late long and severe winter."

So in spite of the bank loss, the Committee had pushed ahead in a confident way with improvements to the school, reflecting perhaps the growing confidence and prosperity of the town.

June 22nd:
Mr. G.S.Dunn was appointed Master in place of Mr. Welch who had resigned in February. Mr. Dunn remained Master for the next twenty-eight years.

August 29th:
"Resolved that for the future the boys leaving the School be supplied with two suits of clothes."

1867
The President for the year was George Dixon, Mayor of Birmingham.

May 31st:
The purchase of twenty-four acres at Sparkbrook, adjoining school lands, for £6,600 was approved. This land lay between Anderton Lane and Warwick Road.

1868   May 1st:
Dr. Bell Fletcher resigned as Honorary Physician after serving the school for twenty-seven years.

1869   May 25th:
"Resolved that Mr. Dunn be permitted to introduce a class for the study of Physiology in combination with Chemistry."

August 24th:
"The Secretary reported that the children and officials of the Institution were entertained by Mr. & Mrs. Cartland at the Priory, King's Heath on Friday last and that the children enjoyed the treat very much. They were conveyed to and from King's Heath by train at the expense of Mr. Cartland."

1870
The Endowed Schools Act of 1869, appointing Commissioners with wide powers to alter existing trusts, had caused some concern to the School Committee. Consequently a scheme was prepared and submitted to the Commissioners in January 1870, detailing any proposed changes from the 1845 arrangements that had obtained Parliamentary and Royal assent. Two main changes were proposed — to alter the residential qualifications for parents to a minimum period of twelve months in Birmingham and to omit the qualification that parents should be practising members of the Church of England.

The second of these changes was fundamental. Until this date the school had been operated on an unswerving policy of adherence to the Anglican church. Only twenty-six years in fact had passed since the Committee had recorded its alarm at the possibility of a body of dissenters obtaining sufficient influence to be able to modify the original purposes of the Charity. Now the change proposed would put the need of the child above all other considerations.

April 22nd:

Mr. Fitch, the Commissioner appointed by the Government to enquire into the state of all the schools for the poorer classes of children in Birmingham, made a report on the school from which these extracts are taken.

"The Blue Coat School in St. Philip's Churchyard is well endowed and admirably managed."

"The order, cheerfulness and mental activity pervading the school on the day of my visit were very striking."

"It is to the credit of the Governors that they have taken every means to avail themselves of the best modern methods and to give instruction of a higher type than would be accessible to the same boys and girls if they had been at National Schools which were exceptionally good."

"The children still wear a costume better suited to that date (1724) than the present."

"On minor points, such as the expediency of retaining an antique and ugly dress, the fairness of excluding the children of Dissenters, or rather of all who do not call themselves members of the Church of England, from the advantages of the institution and the general expediency of maintaining an asylum of this kind for the children, not necessarily of the poor, but of those who can influence the greatest number of subscribers, I am not called upon to express an opinion . . . But granted that its present constitution and aims are right I do not see how those aims could be better or more honourably realised than at present."

November 29th:

"The Committee heard that Mr. Dunn the Head Master has passed an examination at the University of London and has obtained thereby the degree of Bachelor of Arts."

1871   January 30th:

The Endowed Schools Commission outlined their objections to the scheme submitted to them in January 1870. Two of their points were that part of the endowments were used for clothing and that it was not desirable to have a boarding school in the heart of a large city.

They even suggested the possibility of an amalgamation with King Edward's School. All these points were countered in a memorandum prepared by the Committee.

In the early months of this year the *Birmingham Morning News* carried a series of articles on the school. The article of February 21st gave a useful description of the scene inside the school.

The present building is a most commodious one and well adopted in regard to internal arrangements to the accommodation of its numerous inmates. The boys' and girls' dormitories are airy and cheerful looking apartments, the beds being arranged in a double row on either side. They present a very neat appearance, and are kept most scrupulously clean. In close proximity to the boys' dormitories are the masters' bedrooms, so that they may be within hearing should any of the children be taken ill, or disturbance take place, during the night. In the girls' department the same arrangement obtains, the whole of the inmates being thus placed under the immediate personal supervision of those whose duty it is to maintain order and provide for the comfort of those placed under their care. The dining room is a spacious apartment, oblong in shape, with long tables placed down the sides and centre, and presents an interesting, not to say animating appearance, when all the children are seated to partake of the good and substantial meals provided for them. Strict orderliness is rigidly enforced, any lapse from good behaviour always resulting in proportionate punishment for the unfortunate delinquents. There are two school rooms — one for the boys and another for the girls — in which are to be found all the modern appliances for educational purposes. Two rooms are set apart as wardrobes, and all the children are required to keep their clothes tidily, and in the particular place devoted to each. The kitchen, with its brightly kept culinary utensils and range, is large and convenient, and the washhouses and laundry contain all the most recently invented apparata for the saving of labour in this important department. At the back of the building is a large, flagged playground, where the children are allowed to amuse themselves in whatever way they choose during certain hours of the day, being subjected to no other restrictions than those necessary to prevent quarrelsome behaviour, or unfair treatment, by the others of the more juvenile portion of the little community.

1872   November 26th:
This letter was received from the Master.

Revd. Sir,

I beg to ask the assistance of the Committee in purchasing a supply of apparatus for the teaching of Science and that application might be made to the Science Department for the Government aid (50 per cent) towards the purchase of the scientific apparatus marked on the accompanying paper.

The request was approved and £17 spent on apparatus, mainly for magnetism and electricity.

1874
It was now 150 years since the school opened. In 1724 there had been twenty-two boys and ten girls: now there were 151 boys and ninety-six girls. More than 3,500 children had been clothed, maintained and educated inside its walls. Subscriptions now brought in an annual income of £1,400.

1875
The report to the Annual General Meeting pointed out that the present building was inadequate for the number of pupils. In view of the likely increase in value of the Sparkbrook Estate

"Your Committee are of opinion that the time has arrived when an enlargement of the present school should be made by extending it upon the grounds of St. Philip's Rectory or by the erection of a new institution upon the Sparkbrook Estate or some other site."

It was to be over fifty years later that the move to a new site was made.

1876   February 29th:
The Charity Commissioners wrote to say that in accordance with the provisions of the Artisans Dwellings Improvement Act of 1875, the Town Council:

"are proposing to acquire . . . the School buildings belonging to the Blue Coat School with the apparent object of making a new street on the site at present covered by these schools."

The Committee was advised by the Commissioners to negotiate the sale with the Council.

By March, after much correspondence, the Committee had prepared a strong case to present at the Local Inquiry.

"The Mayor thereupon struck out the school property from the compulsory powers of the scheme."

April
The Reverend H.M.Capel said in his report for this year:

"I do not think I have ever found your schools in a better state than at present."

1878   *September 14th:*
The Medical Officer wrote:

"I am sorry to have to report that the cases of cutaneous disease in the school do not diminish but on the contrary are assuming a more serious form."

These skin complaints worried the school authorities who attributed them mainly to overcrowding. The Chairman (Mr. John Cartland) inspected several houses with a view to leasing them to provide extra space. Hamstead Hall was thought to be very suitable. Meantime, the financial situation deteriorated and this idea had to be abandoned. Fortunately the health of the children gradually improved.

October 29th:
Elementary French was introduced to the curriculum for the older boys.

1879   *April 22nd:*
The Hon. A.C.G.Calthorpe accepted the office of President for the coming year.

1876 – 1880 Notes on these years by a scholar of the time

Headmaster: George Dunn Esq. B.A

Two other masters, two mistresses for the girls, a Matron, a Nurse, Kitchen staff etc.

There were about 150 boys and 90 girls. They got up at 6 a.m. summer and 6.30 in the winter. Lessons began at 9.00 a.m. till 12 or 12.30 and from 2 until 4 and from 6 until 7.30. There were no lessons on Saturday, which was Inspection Day for Clothing and all cleaning materials. All the children had allotted jobs of cleaning to do. All rooms were cleaned thoroughly once a fortnight, and that morning the children got up at 5.30 a.m.

The Masters had older boys to wait on them, fetch meals etc.

Meals:

Breakfast	usually bread and dripping and milk
Dinner	occasionally meat with potatoes,
	or rice pudding only
	or bread and treacle only
	or bread and cheese only
	on Sundays suet pudding with salt only
Supper	mostly bread and treacle and water. Coffee
	was sometimes given on special occasions,
	but the children never had tea, sugar or
	green vegetables.

Punishments (apart from corporal) included cleaning the girls' Sunday shoes, cleaning knives and forks, and scrubbing four flights of stairs. These were punishments given for such things as talking during meal times or making too much noise.

Tradesmen and Farmers would often offer money to the children but they were punished if they were caught accepting it.

They attended Church (St. Philip's) three times on Sunday and there was an organised long walk twice a week. The bath was large enough to hold twenty at a time and they could swim in it.

Rigid discipline was relaxed on some occasions, and once when the playing yard was flooded and then frozen over, the Head-master skated with the boys.

1881   May 31st:
> "The Committee had under consideration the desirability of the boys in the school being allowed to go to the Northwood St. Baths with the view of their learning to swim."

It was arranged that a class should go each Tuesday at 11.30.

> *September 27th:*
> "The Deputy Chairman brought before the Committee the desirability of carrying out the Minute of the School Committee as to providing a fund to enable boys after leaving the school to attend the evening classes of Sir Josiah Mason's College. Resolved that this matter be approved."

1883   March 30th:
The A.G.M. reported on the Science classes:

> "These classes contained about 50 boys of whom 47 were presented for examination in Electricity, Chemistry and Physiology . . . Of the 116 certificates gained, 19 were in the advanced stages of Physiology and Electricity."

Train up a child in
the way he fhould go
and when he is old he
will not depart from it

We cannot recompence
you but ye fhall be
recompenced at the
refurrection of the juft

Samuel Grubb's statues designed to go over the School door.

The school today.

1885   February 25th:
A statement of facts was sent to the Charity Commissioners in London, as a first step towards obtaining their approval to the sale of the present school and its transfer to a more suitable site. The area of land in question was 1,360 sq yds. held on the 1722 lease and 1,000 sq. yds. freehold.

July 28th:
The Charity Commissioners stated their unwillingness to consider the sale of the site until new regulations had been agreed and said they were not prepared to undertake this work for the time being.

September 29th:
"Perambulation of the School Estates by the Estate Committee. On Friday September 18th the members of the Estate Committee were invited by their Chairman, Mr. T.S. Fallows to dine with him and Mrs. Fallows at their house 19 Calthorpe Road. . . . After dinner the whole of the gentlemen present with the exception of Mr. Cartland, proceeded in one of R.L.Hunt's omnibuses to view the school estate . . . The Committee have to report that they found the property of

The school today – the chapel.

the Charity in a satisfactory state and were altogether much pleased with their visit."

1886 September 28th:
"Resolved that the sincere thanks of this Committee be presented to Mr. John Holder for his kind present to the boys in the school of 6 cricket bats, 3 sets of wickets, 4 balls, 1 pair leg guards, 1 pair wicket keeper's gloves, 1 pair batting gloves and 1 bag."

1888 April 24th:
"Resolved that the warmest thanks of this Committee be presented to the former pupil of the school (a girl) who on the 5th instant gave the handsome donation of one hundred pounds."

1889 August 27th
"Resolved that the Estate Committee be requested to ascertain if the leasehold portion of the School site can be enfranchised and at what cost the Ground rent of 10s. a year payable to the Rector of St. Philip's can be discharged."

1890 April 11th:
At the A.G.M. mention was made of:

"The offer of one of their number, Mr. John Holder, to give about 7 acres of most valuable land on which to erect any new buildings."

A meeting of subscribers on October 13th of this year passed a resolution approving the sale of the present site and the transfer of the school to a new position. There were several problems involved, the first being to secure, if possible, the freehold of the land leased from the Rector of St. Philip's. This would make the site more valuable when it was offered for sale and also offer more freedom to a buyer for development of the area. Also the Charity Commission in London, who controlled the financial assets of the School, had to be won over in support of the plan. A suitable new site had to be found and bought, plans prepared and approved and a buyer found for the old site. The elimination of these problems and the upheavals of the 1914 – 1918 war, postponed the move for a further forty years.

The School Badge (see Appendix D)

11

1891 – 1920
A New School Site is Found

1891 February 24th:
> "The Draft of the agreement on the proposed sale and purchase of the Ground rent of 10s. a year and reversion in fee of the school site which was leasehold having been submitted by the Solicitors to the Committee, resolved that the Solicitors be instructed to settle and approve same."

This 1891 agreement proved to be abortive and it was another twenty years before the freehold of the land was finally secured. On the assumption however, that the agreement would be successfully negotiated, the Committee met the Assistant Commissioner appointed by the Charity Commissioners to enquire into the reasons for the suggested transfer of the school to a different site.

1892 May 31st:
A draft Scheme for the future government of the school had been received from the Charity Commission. This scheme was looked at carefully and the Committee sent a reply in which they objected to many of the clauses. After further correspondence, the Commission gave way on several minor points, but stood their ground on other matters that to the school were of great importance. In particular the school governors were not prepared to restrict the number of pupils to 250, nor were they willing to apply part of the endowment funds to establishing Exhibition scholarships at a place of higher education as required by the Commissioners. On December 27th, the Committee decided to request a public meeting to protest against the high handed approach of the Charity Commissioners and the Mayor of Birmingham fixed the day for the town's protest meeting as Wednesday January 18th, 1893.

1893
An account of the meeting in the Town Hall can be read in the *Birmingham Daily Gazette* of 19th January, 1893. The Mayor signed a resolution opposing the Charity Commissioners' scheme and there was unanimous support for the following resolution:

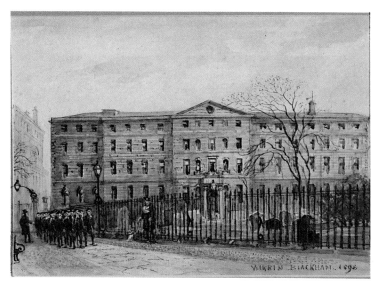

This watercolour, painted in 1898 by G. Warren Blackham, is owned by the Birmingham City Museum.

"That this meeting protests against the limitation of the number of poor children of Birmingham who may be clothed, lodged, maintained and educated in the Blue Coat School of this city, as proposed by the scheme prepared by the Charity Commissioners and to the proposed diversion of any portion of the funds of this school from such a purpose, to the establishment of a Day School and the compulsory maintenance of Exhibitions at places of higher education."

This resolution of protest hardly conveyed the full measure of the support for the school's stand. The difference of opinion had stirred civic pride in one of its most prized institutions and a determination that this institution, inspired and financed for nearly 200 years by Birmingham citizens, should not be tampered with by outsiders, even if the outsiders were an official government body. Apart from the Mayor, there were others whose support for the school was of great consequence. Mr. Joseph Chamberlain was unable to attend the meeting but he wrote:

"Any support which I can give to your protest, in or out of Parliament, will be most heartily afforded."

The Rt. Hon. Jesse Collings M.P., talking of the Charity Commissioners said:

"They were six gentlemen in London . . . but unfortunately they had added to that good work a desire to meddle where they were not wanted."

Mr. Walter Showell:

"He humorously suggested that Mr. P.A.Muntz M.P. should move for a committee to sit upon the Charity Commissioners in the shape of a 'De Lunatico Inquirendo'. (Laughter)."

Mr. Powell Williams M.P.:

"He said a more gratuitous and preposterous interference with a charity of a great city was never, he believed, yet perpetuated . . . He regretted that the Governors of the School had ever approached the Charity Commissioners for it was like putting a penny in the Commissioners' slot and receiving an earthquake."

The Charity Commission displayed good sense under this assault and on January 25th requested copies of the newspapers in which the meeting had been reported. Sensitive to the strength of public indignation that was evident, the Commissioners notified the school on March 6th that they were prepared to withdraw the restrictions on pupil numbers and were willing to meet the Governors' wishes on most of the disputed points. Finally, by November 1893, the Commission had conceded all the main points at issue apart from the vesting of the school property in the Commission instead of Trustees. There can be no doubt that the stubborn tactics of the school authorities protected and kept intact the particular nature and character of the school.

March 28th:
Mr. Dunn resigned. He was replaced by Mr. G. Gill in May, but after an illness the latter resigned in August 1894.

1894   July 31st:
Lord Dudley, President for this year, offered as much land as was required for a new school on his Himley estate but this was thought to be too far away from the city. Possible sites at Acock's Green, King's Heath, Stechford, King's Norton and Olton were inspected.

December 4th:
Mr. John Irving was appointed Headmaster.

1896   November 24th:
A fifteen acres site at Olton was finally approved for the new school and an agreement made on the purchase price. The land

was situated 600 yds. from Olton railway station and five miles from the city.

1897   July 20th:

The Charity Commission gave its consent to the purchase of the land at Olton. On November 2nd, two notice boards were fixed on the land, one facing the Great Western Railway, the other facing Warwick Road, announcing it as the future site of the Blue Coat School. Earlier in the year, on February 27th, the paragraphs below had been printed in the *Weekly Post*.

The Looker-on

A good deal of anxious curiosity is being manifested in capitalist and speculative circles as to the ultimate disposal of the site on which the Blue Coat School now stands. When the school is removed to its new home at Olton, the old building and the land, it is well known, will be sold, and I understand the property will go to the highest bidder. It will certainly be the most interesting auction held in Birmingham for a great many years. I have heard that one Gentleman would be quite willing to pay £30,000 for the property, but it is worth more than that, and there is an impression that the hammer will fall at a figure much nearer £50,000. When the property is sold what will the site be utilised for? Shops can scarcely be erected with a frontage to the churchyard. The best suggestion I have heard yet is that the Ecclesiastical Commissioners should become the purchasers. If Birmingham ever becomes a Bishopric, it is almost a foregone conclusion that St. Philip's Church will be the cathedral. In that case the rectory would form a capital deanery, and the site on which the Blue Coat School stands would make a most convenient cathedral close, with ample space for the erection of residences and offices for the cathedral staff.

1898

As well as causing speculation about the use of the land on which the school now stood, the likely disappearance of a familiar landmark from the city centre provoked extra interest in the school. The *Birmingham Mercury* of December 12th 1898, carried this article:

Within a short period of time the Blue Coat School of Birmingham will have closed its doors, and the Blue Coat boy in his swallow-tail coat, muffin cap, and corded knicker-bockers, will have removed to more healthy surroundings.

We know that the removal will be for his good, but we regret his departure as that of an old familiar friend, whose presence in the city has always been welcome. But ere the place is closed and the boys have gone Mr. Walter J. Morgan R.B.A., has taken the opportunity of painting the school, and has produced a work that lovers of art will value for its own sake, the lovers of Birmingham for the local interests and sentiments which it expresses. We have before us a proof of the photogravure from the picture. The Blue Coat School is painted as it is to-day, the point of view being near the north-east corner of St. Philip's Churchyard, so that nearly the whole of the frontage is seen. From beneath the ancient doorway a troop of Blue Coat boys are issuing, on church-going bent. The ostensible comfort of their lives, as seen in their healthy faces, is a speaking illustration of the blessing of the charity under which they have been reared and educated. Contrasting with them are a couple of wan street arabs, who certainly have greater originality of expression, but whose ragged clothing and hungry look, indicate only too plainly the hardships of their life. We cannot approve of the attitude of the girl who is resting her head on her brother's shoulder, but possibly the artist's excuse would be the necessity of emphasising the difference between the two groups of children. A young boy of graceful figure, holding a little girl by the hand, stands aside to let the troop go by. Mr. Morgan has produced a fine and powerful picture, bold and generous in its conception, and executed with faithfulness and loving care. The tale that it tells is the finest appeal that has yet been made on behalf of the Blue Coat School.

1899   August 26th:

The renewal of interest was continued in the *Mercury* in a much longer article of this date, from which these extracts are taken:

One of the Happy Homes of the World

I spent half-a-day with them six years ago; they were happy then, just as they are happy now; 'they' of course, meaning the species, not the individual, for I suppose that every scholar I saw in 1893 has flown away from the nest, and advisedly. The children love it; of that there can be no doubt. The Birmingham Blue Coat School is one of the happy homes of the world. You cannot walk round about it and tell the towers thereof, without coming to the conclusion that, taking one consideration with another, the Bluecoat

The Walter Morgan painting. The original hangs in the Dining Hall. There is a lithograph copy in the entrance lobby of the Administration Block.

scholar's lot is quite a happy one. You shall walk from one end of England to another and not find a happier, merrier, finer looking hundred and fifty boys. You shall peregrinate from the rising of the sun unto the going down of the same and not see a cleaner, sweeter, more delightful hundred girls. It cannot be denied that the institution is a charity, but if every charity were like this, there would be no reproach in the term. The scholars are under no stigma; they feel none; they come back to the school year after year as to a beloved home; they keep up correspondence with the teachers, as with dear and faithful friends; they do not conceal their bringing up, on the contrary, they are proud of it, and expect to be more highly valued by reason of the connection. When a scholar leaves for a situation he or she is provided with two complete suits, two of everything they can wear, and a Bible and a Prayer Book; these last called 'leaving books' and prized through life. After a year in one situation the Bluecoat School makes a girl a present of five shillings; after two years, seven and sixpence; after three years ten shillings and a certificate. The children are not treated as paupers. There is no grinding subservience; no Bumbledom; no freezing dole of eleemosynary bread; no squalid stinting; no moral degradation of any kind. Nor is there any waste. The arts of happiness are carefully studied. The joys of home are systematised . . .

Nor do they ever forget the suet puddings, word of magic to a Bluecoat scholar! For be it known to a listening world that THE SUET PUDDINGS OF THE SCHOOL are alone, are *sui generis*, unapproachable, like no other puddings that ever were, are, or are to be. Being steamed, not boiled in the usual way, they are brown, like plum puddings, savoury and flavoury, and withal, as light as an exhalation. At Mr. Bolton's yearly reception this ancient dish is first in favour; the old boys and girls who re-visit the glimpses of the school would not be at home without the beloved suet pudding. Letters from India, Australia, from China to Peru, while announcing prosperity and general satisfaction, ruefully admit that the suet puddings of these countries leave much to be desired. The bill of fare in Mr. Bolton's room has roast mutton, beef, milk and bread, with stewed fruit and all other things conformable, but none of them are reckoned to be a patch on suet puddings. Accordingly, this luxury is reserved for Sunday, the day of festival, the first day of the week in more senses than one.

October 3rd:
Five gold medals were presented by two former pupils. One of them was to be awarded annually to the best behaved boy. Sir John Holder donated £20 to buy similar medals for the girls. The first boy to receive one of these medals was Leonard Cottrell. At the end of five years the donors were to review the position and decide then whether to continue the awards.

1900 *November 27th:*
Mr. Irving resigned after six years as Headmaster. Unusually, he was re-appointed Headmaster in 1912 and served in this post for a further fifteen years.

1901 *January 25th:*
Mr. T.J.Turned was appointed Headmaster.

July 2nd:
Two legacies were received — one of £1,000 from Mr. John Bayliss, the other of £500 from Mr. Samuel Tonks, a former Governor.

1902 *January 28th:*
After 25 years service on the committee, Mr. J.H. Stone resigned as Chairman, owing to ill health. Stone prizes are still awarded annually on Prize-Giving Day from a memorial fund.

October 28th:
An agreement was made to hire rooms in Steelhouse Lane, adjacent to the Ebenezer Chapel, on an annual basis, in order to relieve the pressure on dormitory accommodation.

During this year the Rt. Hon. Jesse Collings M.P. had been active in London on the school's behalf. As a result, the Charity Commissioners' powers over the school had been transferred to the Board of Education. I think it would be extremely difficult to maintain that this move conferred any real benefit on the school, either in the short term or over a long period. No doubt however, the Governors who had experienced the frustrating interference of the Charity Commissioners in the last ten years, or had learned of it from others, felt much satisfaction at being delivered from their hands.

1903 *May 19th:*
Mr. Turned had either resigned or worse, since Mr. E.T.Philips was appointed Headmaster at £150 per year.

The School at Play. c.1910.

May 26th:
Eleven years after the initial attempt to purchase the freehold of the 1722 land had met with failure, the school began moves to re-open the negotiations. At this time (1903), the Rector of St. Philip's was also the Bishop of Coventry. His solicitor stressed the valid point that the lease granted by the Reverend William Higgs had been for the specific purpose of erecting a school, and that the school now wished to obtain the freehold in order to be in a position to sell the site more profitably. Obviously this was the case and the church authorities felt no urgency to conclude an agreement.

December 29th:
The school received a legacy of £5,000 from Mr. Thomas Best.

1904   March 17th:
Mr. Philips resigned and was replaced by Mr. H. Cleave the following month. The latter stayed only two years and was succeeded in 1906 by Mr. Wm. Howes. Since the retirement of Mr. Dunn in 1893, there had been no fewer than six Headmasters in the short period of twelve years. The right kind of man may have been difficult to find, since the post was exacting and required dedication. Equally, the requirement that the Head-

The School at Work. c.1910.

master should be a bachelor, or that if married, should have no family, was a very limiting factor and probably accounts for this rapid turnover. Certainly the issue was not that of the Head-master's salary, which compared favourably at all times with the terms offered by other schools in different parts of the country.

1905 – 1909

A considerable amount of negotiation took place during these years, as the School Governors attempted to solve the problems involved in the transfer of the school to a new site. At one time it seemed possible that the Colmore Row site would be bought by the Ecclesiastical Commissioners, but various difficulties pre-vented this from happening.

1909   December7th:

Rooms over 99/100 Bull Street were rented to provide extra sleeping accommodation for thirty boys.

1910   March 22nd:

The offer made by the Governors to purchase the freehold of the land leased from the Rector of St. Philip's was accepted by the Ecclesiastical Commissioners. The price agreed was £5,000 and the purchase was completed in November 1911.

The essential step towards realising the plans for a new school had been made. Now the whole site could be offered freehold (one

The School Dining Hall. c.1910.

of the few remaining freehold sites in the city centre) at a price
that would cover the cost of rebuilding at Olton. It is interesting
to note that the Board of Education had advised the Governors
to hold out for a figure below that set by the Ecclesiastical
Commissioners. Later circumstances were to show that this was
a very modest sum to have paid for the freehold. In any case the
negotiations had already lasted twenty years, had broken down
once in 1891, and the last thing the Governors would have wanted
was a second breakdown.

1912

Early this year forty-one architects (an impressive number)
entered a competition to provide the best design for the new
school. From their comments on the difficulties presented by the
nature of the site at Olton, it was thought advisable to review the
advantages and disadvantages of building on it. A portion of the
land had been acquired compulsorily by the Great Western
Railway, shortly after its purchase by the school in 1897. This
reduction of the area lessened the advantages of the site and
finally:

> *March 26th:*
> "Resolved that after the overwhelming evidence received as
> to the unsuitability of the site at Olton, efforts be made to

The girls' playground in 1910.

secure a new site as soon as possible and if practicable the same should be in the area of Greater Birmingham."

July 30th:
A letter was received from the Calthorpe Estate agent:

"I am authorised to say that the Hon. Mrs. Anstruther-Gough-Calthorpe, with the concurrence of her Trustees Surveyor, is prepared to sell, subject to existing tenancies, a site at the junction of Harborne Hill and Metchley Lane and extending along the Somerset Road for the erection of the proposed new School buildings. . . . The area is 17 acres and the price would be £7,500 (including Holly Cottage and its site). I would point out that the price named is a low one and has been fixed with the desire of assisting the school."

Needless to say, the offer of this splendid, freehold site at such a low price answered all the Committee's problems and the purchase was completed in 1913. So the two vital steps had been taken towards the goal of moving the school. The old site could be sold freehold and a new site in a prime position had been obtained. To complete a run of good fortune, on the day the purchase of the Edgbaston site was completed, the Committee learned of a legacy of £10,000 from Mr. John Roderick.

1913   March 18th:
"Mr. Alderman Ansell reported that he had had a chat with the President (Sir Benjamin Stone) who was willing to accept the office of President provided arrangements could be made for laying the Foundation Stone of the New Building during his term of office."

April 9th:
Twenty-three sets of plans for the New School were submitted to the Assessors, Mr. Bateman, Mr. Hunt and Mr. Silk. The plans chosen finally were those of Mr. J.L.Ball of Paradise Street, estimated to cost £65,725.

August 12th:
The Visitors' Book must have been mislaid, for on this date there appears in the Committee Minute Book, the signature of the King of Buganda and of his chiefs!

August 26th:
"The Secretary reported that the President entertained the children at the site at Edgbaston on Tuesday last."

A photograph of this treat, taken by Sir Benjamin, is kept at the school. Although it was taken nearly eighty years ago it is an excellent photograph and in good condition. Messrs. Ansell, Barrows, Bryson, Cartland, Edwards, Heaton and Shaw, all Governors of the school, appear on the photograph.

1914 – 1919
The years 1914 – 1919 contained little of interest in the school's history, in contrast to the awesome events of the first world war. Ordinary routine was maintained but the war postponed the scheme for re-building at Harborne. Part of the site was in fact leased to the City Council during this period to be used as allotments to increase the home production of food.

12
Notes of a Former Scholar
1920 – 1925

These notes were written in 1961 and are repeated as they were written.

Years 1920 – 1925

Sunday:	Breakfast	Bread and Milk and salt in pewter vessel
	Dinner	Corned Beef. Bread, Orange
	Tea	Bread, Margarine, Tea
Monday:	Breakfast	Bread and milk, salt
	Dinner	Roast Beef, Cabbage, Jacket Potato, Gravy
	Tea	Bread and one tablespoonful Jam, Cocoa
Tuesday:	Breakfast	Porridge & salt
	Dinner	Stew
	Tea	Bread & Jam & Tea
Wednesday:	Breakfast	Bread & Milk & Salt
	Dinner	Boiled Butter Beans
	Tea	Bread & Jam, Cocoa (during summer, sometimes lettuce and possibly pickled walnut)
Thursday:	Breakfast	Bread & Milk & Salt
	Dinner	Boiled Rice & Treacle (Dark Type)
	Tea	Bread & Jam, Tea
Friday:	Breakfast	Porridge & Milk & Salt
	Dinner	Slice of Bread. Covered with toasted cheese
	Tea	Bread & Treacle, Tea or Cocoa

Saturday:	Breakfast	Bread & Milk & Salt
	Dinner	'Podge' a poor imitation of a boiled pudding with currants in it, hated by all.
	Tea	Bread & Jam, rare occasions, Lemon Cheese

These meals never varied for the first two years I was in the Blue Coat School, in Colmore Row. Except perhaps, when about every month for some reason we might have a slice of currant cake. I believe a generous governor decided on occasions it was time we had some. Even so, serious illness was almost unknown, and all the children were plump and healthy, when the time came to leave the school at 14 (boys) and 15 (girls). Girls were kept on always, to learn domestic service, they did not attend school, they had left school, but learned duties in the home, cleaning, laundry, waiting at table, and general duties of a house-maid. Which, of course, must have been a boon, as regards staff and salaries.

After a Governors' meeting, about the year 1921, one or two of these gentlemen, came among us children, it may have been Mr. Bryson or Mr. Viney, it would have been typical of either, and asked us our likes and dislikes in our diet. With a child on his knee, Mr. Bryson asked his questions, we all as one hated margarine. Funnily enough, we never had it again, it was always luscious butter, such as we've never tasted since. That children of such a tender age would even know the difference amazes me now.

Wednesdays:

We had a half day from lessons. At 2 o'clock, we set out to walk, in line, two by two, for the New Site at Harborne. Little girls in front, and so on along the line, to the big girls of 14 at the end. Our straw-brimmed hats, held on with elastic under the chin, and our capes, neatly folded over our arms, in case of rain. The boys were not far behind, or in front, by about 15 minutes. They were absolutely wonderful to see, the Cold Stream Guards had nothing on them when it came marching in unison. I would think so, the way they were drilled as soon as they entered the school. The girls did not march, we were little ladies, but the boys' legs and feet moved as one. Our route was — Colmore Row, Victoria Square, Paradise Street, Broad Street, Five Ways, Harborne Lane. On reaching this point, word was passed along the line, 'we can talk now'. One mistress and prefects were in charge of this journey.

There was a tennis court, where some of the girls houses are to-day, and sometimes another mistress would come along to play tennis with the mistress on duty, but children were never allowed to play, and how I would have loved to learn. We just roamed around the field and in the orchards, but we did enjoy ourselves nevertheless. We had a cup of cold milk and a piece of bread and butter, then we set off for the long walk back to Colmore Row. Incidentally, dense traffic was almost unknown then. Again, we could talk until we reached Five Ways, then care had to be taken in crossing roads, or we might get run over — by a horse or bicycle.

We had Annual Sports Day, when we went by train, to Monument Lane and then walked to Harborne. No parents were allowed or invited, it was just children, masters and mistresses. We had prizes for racing events, and tug of war, Milk, bread and butter and cake. The train ride back was a happy one, when we sang loudly, 'Jolly good luck to the driver for bringing us safely home'. Again we were not allowed to mingle with the boys, we were entirely separate, if my memory serves me right.

About the year 1922 – 1923 it was decided we had a monthly half-day (on a Wednesday) with our own individual families, at home. We left school at 2 o'clock and promised faithfully to be back indoors at 7 o'clock. It was wonderful. We travelled to and fro by tram-car. What stories we had to tell when we arrived back.

Educational lessons were taken at the Old Ebenezer Chapel in Steelhouse Lane. We walked two by two, every day, for lessons at the rear of the chapel, where there were some excellent classrooms. About year 1923, new school rooms were built, at the home, above the girls' playground, henceforth no need to go to Ebenezer. But, the walk was gone. So, to overcome this, at a quarter to nine every morning we walked, again in line, along Colmore Row, around the cathedral, along Temple Row, through the churchyard, and so, back to school and in our desks, for nine o'clock.

Underneath these classrooms was situated the swimming bath, which served also as washing baths, for both boys and girls, on Saturdays and Fridays. Once a month was wash head night for girls, when, a mistress would bring along a balloon, and did we have fun. We lined up to walk down the steps to the water, each taking a piece of soap, Sunlight, with us, and as we came out again we had to turn around in front of the mistress, lift up our feet, to ensure we were clean! Swimming lessons were given during school lesson time, with the mistress walking the plank, calling 'In, Out, In, Out'. I personally hated it, but would have adored to learn tennis or have piano lessons, but, these activities were never thought of, strangely enough. Games in the school yard consisted of Basket Ball and King Ball, and also rounders and cricket. Again, I was most unhappy at this, and would hide away with a book. However I finished up alright as Head Prefect and generally voted by all the girls 'The Best Girl' and duly given a guinea prize, which I treasure today. 'The Best Boy' prize went to Frederick Derby, who left the school twelve months before me, and is doing very well for himself at the Delta Metal Company, in Birmingham. I believe, he has been there ever since he left the Blue Coat School. Another extremely clever boy was Frederick Andrews, also, employed at the same place with very good positions. Our clever girl was Ethel Govier, our Bessie Bunter was Nancy Freeman, our expelled girl was Betty Turpie, who ran away, she hired a taxi side-car, from Temple Row, and said 'Pay at the other end' and was brought back from Handsworth, 'sent to Coventry' and duly expelled.

Medicines were weekly doses of brimstone and treacle, and Calamel tablets and Sulpher tablets. During winter, a Melrose tablet was handed to each child to keep in use on chilblains, if very painful, they were painted with iodine which had a tendency to dry the skin, causing the chilblain to crack, fingers and heels were sorry sights during the winter time.

Every child from the age of nine, the youngest age in those days, had a job to do, after rising from bed at 6 a.m. The only job I remember we did not do, was clean windows, an outside man was engaged for this. Every mistresses and masters bedroom was cleaned and left spic and span, every morning by a girl. Every night, this girl had to go into said bedroom and turn down the quilt, take chamber from cupboard and place under the bed. At 6 a.m. each morning this girl would place can of hot water outside the mistresses bedroom, collect the shoes left there to be cleaned. The same was done for matron, house-governor etc. Taps on all basins, on top floors, at end of corridors, sparkled, at six thirty in the morning.

Every month we had our particular chore changed. Sweeping out the back hall, six steps. These famous steps were so old, they had a big dip in the centre, and must have been in continual use ever since 1724, which would make it two hundred years. Back hall, play-room, boot-room, cloak-room, outside lavatories, outside brush-cupboard. Saturday morning, brushes, hand brooms, step-ladders and dustpans and dusters had to be scrubbed, shining white. Then we stood in line, to have them passed. Saturdays we stood in line, in back hall, for stores, this was your requirements for your particular job. A small amount of soap, soft soap, soda, Ronuk, Blacking and dusters. The boot-room girl, would collect her quota of blacking, find a tin lid, and away to the boot-room (beside the swimming bath) place a small quantity in lid and mix with water. Girls then lined up to dip the brush in and then polish their boots till they shone. In this same room every Saturday morning, nurse would proceed to tooth-comb every girl's head with metholated spirits, the disgrace was terrible if she found a dirty head. Report to Matron, as she was coming from the staff dining room. "Go and wash your head, and come back next week, after you have written out a thousand lines, 'A Blue Coat School girl must keep her head clean'." A shortened version would not do, such as 'A B.C.S. girl' it had to be done like this:

A Blue Coat School girl must keep her head clean	*This was*
A Blue Coat School girl must keep her head clean	*done in*
A Blue Coat School girl must keep her head clean	*groups of*
A Blue Coat School girl must keep her head clean	*ten until a*
A Blue Coat School girl must keep her head clean	*thousand*
A Blue Coat School girl must keep her head clean	*was*
A Blue Coat School girl must keep her head clean	*completed.*

Remember there were no ball pens, we had to dip into the ink pot, and by the time the thousand lines were completed, fingers and thumbs were black and blue.

   Should a girl break a cup or plate, she stood with broken article, down the hall, wait for matron, who told her she would forfeit her penny-worth of sweets to pay for it. One of the chores for the younger girls was to be chamber-girl. Two used to work together emptying and washing and placing beneath the individual beds. If she was unfortunate enough to break one, the humiliation of standing in the back hall with the offending article, was worse than going without the penny-worth of sweets. By the way, we all had our small amounts of money in the bank, given us by generous friends from home. Two girls, (prefects), every Saturday at noon, would go out to buy about sixty penny-worth's of boiled sweets. If anyone preferred, they could sacrifice their sweets and buy a birthday card to send home, but could not do both. For these, the prefects went to Woolworth's in the Bull Ring.

Sunday mornings we had an extra half-hour in bed, getting up at 6.30 a.m. If confirmed, older girls attended Holy Communion service at the cathedral, at 8 a.m. Morning service was attended by everyone at 11a.m. The B.C.S children always sat upstairs in the gallery, attended by the master and mistress on duty. We also had to attend afternoon service at 3 p.m. Once a month, for a change, we attended St. Martin's Church in the Bull Ring, sitting in the front side seats, we must have looked very picturesque. During all these various activities, girls and boys were never ever allowed to speak to each other or anyone of the opposite sex.

Every week boots were inspected for repair, if one boot needed attention you searched a huge box, to find matching boot to wear for a week or fortnight, if you were unsuccessful, then you had to wear two left boots or right boots, whichever the case might be, until your own one came back.

The laundry was at Harborne, ruled over by the Laundry mistress, who lived out. Every week, about four older girls, who of course did not attend school, having left school, as such, 14 – 15 yrs of age, would travel in the school van to Harborne, and from 9 a.m. until 5 p.m. would stand ironing, tipits*, aprons, caps, handkerchiefs and endless numbers of shirts. Woe betide you if you scorched anything. The laundry mistress always did staff laundry. She seldom smiled and ruled with a rod of iron. Tablecloths she ironed, they were stiff with starch and sparkled like glass when finished, and staff shirts and blouses.

The only staff at Colmore Row consisted of House-Governor (Headmaster) four masters (two lived in, two lived out) Matron, Asst. Matron, two mistresses — all lived in. One house-maid, Bertha, lived in. Secretary lived out and so did the porter. On the first floor, overlooking the churchyard, were several rooms reserved for House-Governor and his wife, and, sometimes their son. They were attended by one of the older girls and she became more or less, their own maid, serving them early morning tea in

---

*   See Glossary, Appendix G.

bed, to last thing at night with supper. I myself was in demand quite a lot for these duties, which I enjoyed immensely.

We were visited periodically by a dentist, all had teeth examined and attended to, if required. All children not vaccinated, parents were contacted for reasons, and were duly vaccinated and wore a red ribbon round the arm. Illness, real illness, was never known.

Punishments for boys consisted of going outside the classroom, bending down, first turning tail-coats up, and six of the best, with the cane.

Christmas was a child's dream come true, we had everything. Turkey, Xmas Pudding, Xmas trees, Santa Claus. A present, a party, where we mixed with the boys, but we were too shy to appreciate this. We visited Theatre Royal and Alexandra, for Pantomimes. Looking back, it was not all bad, some of it was rather wonderful,

On leaving the school girls at age of 15, and boys at 14, we were given a full outfit, consisting of smart dress, coat, hat, shoes, gloves and complete change of underwear. Similar for the boys. It was a wonderful thrill, we were completely changed, in a flash we seemed to be adults!

A position was found, either in an office, or domestic service, whichever we preferred, if service, girls were also given necessary uniform, caps, aprons etc.

Governors presented us with a beautiful bible, prayer book, and another book, entitled *Helps to the study of the Bible*. And so we were launched!

Irene Johnson
1961

13

1920 – 1930
The Last Ten Years in St. Philip's Place, including the Bi-centenary

While the information and facts for this comparatively recent period were obtained from the written records, annual reports and press coverage, it was possible (particularly in 1961 – 1963 when this was first written), to supplement these official sources with the personal recollections of a number of people who had been associated with the school. Mr. F.H. Viney, who was elected a Governor of the school as far back as 1922, was one of those whose deep regard for the school and its children, and long service to the school brought warmth and humanity to statistics and figures, such as the fact that on December 31st, 1920, there were 125 boys and seventy-seven girls on the register. The Headmaster was Mr. John Irving and the unexpected rise in the costs of running the school was a factor that further complicated the difficult and urgent decision faced by the Governors — whether to keep the school going in Colmore Row or to move it as soon as possible to Harborne.

There was no ready answer to this question. If the school stayed in its present premises, a fairly large sum of money would have to be spent on improvements to the buildings. For some years the Colmore Row building had lacked the capacity to provide teaching and sleeping accommodation for all the pupils. As has been noted earlier, some of the boys slept in rented rooms in Bull Street, and most of the girls were taught in the classrooms at the Ebenezer Chapel in Steelhouse Lane. Under the terms of the 1918 Education Act, however, the school would not be able to apply (successfully that is) for official recognition as an Institution School, without being able to show that the premises in Colmore Row were adequate to meet all the needs of its pupils, educational and domestic. The alternative solution, of organising a fairly hasty move to Harborne, was, on examination, unrealistic. It was essential to sell the Colmore Row site at the best possible price in order to cover the building costs at Harborne. A quick sale was unlikely to fetch the best price. Then there were the requirements of agreeing the plans for the new school, obtaining tenders, and at the end of all this, waiting for the buildings to be ready for occupation. The final discouragement for this solution was the high cost of building. So the decision was taken to spend money on the Colmore Row building, a decision that determined inevitably, that the old site would have to be used for a few more years.

1921

"The whole of the present buildings were surveyed and in view of the high cost of building it was decided to reconstruct the existing premises in order to bring them more up to date, rather than embark on a costly building at Harborne. . . . Holly Cottage on the Harborne site has been converted into an Infirmary with a Laundry attached. . . . The rooms at Bull Street have been given up: notice to terminate the occupation of classrooms at Ebenezer Chapel has been served; and as soon as the alterations have been completed, the School will be once again a self contained Institution."

Just over £6,000 had to be spent on the alterations and improvements mentioned above, mainly at the Harborne site.

1922

The alterations to the school were fairly extensive and involved some disturbance to the school routine. To allow the contractor, Messrs. Whittall, to begin work without disrupting the school programme, the children were given an extended holiday at Easter, leaving the school on April 12th and not returning until May 17th. In addition to the bill for the alterations (£9,665), the school decided to pay all the parents 5s. a week for each of the three extra weeks that the children were at home. So the new classrooms were opened officially by the Lord Mayor of Birmingham, President of the school, on October 4th and the Annual Report also announced that:

"At Harborne the Governors have regained possession of land recently used as allotments and by this means land has been put under cultivation to provide vegetables for the School. A new Lodge has been built for the occupation of the Gardener, and entrance gates have been erected; the playing fields have been extended and a belt of trees has been planted."

Mr. Cyril Marsh, well known to hundreds of Blue Coats, was engaged to look after the Harborne site. He occupied the new Lodge until his retirement in 1976.

1924

"The old buildings of Harborne House having been pulled down, the Governors considered it necessary to provide a Sports Pavilion where the children can shelter in wet weather on their usual visits. The new Pavilion has been completed. . . . The children visit the playing field on Saturdays as often as possible during the summer months, in addition to its use for organised games."

"It is common knowledge that negotiations have been in progress for the sale of the present site of the School. . . . But the circumstances of recent years have made the removal more difficult for a variety of reasons, and expenditure on the present buildings has prolonged their usefulness."

More than one offer for the Colmore Row site was received. One in particular, an offer of £100,000, was pursued over several months but was abandoned eventually when the Ecclesiastical Commissioners refused to modify the restrictions on the freehold to enable the purchasers to erect a residential hotel with a liquor licence.

Curiously, the bicentenary of the School passed without enthusiasm, or indeed, mention. The General Minutes contain no reference to the fact that it was 200 years since the School opened, and it is entirely possible, no other explanation being offered, even in the minutes of the sub-committees, that the significance of the date went unnoticed. The same silence was observed in the local press. So a notable landmark in the affairs of the School neither attracted nor received any attention.

1925

There were 104 boys and sixty girls in the School.

"It is with special pleasure that the Governors record the receipt of a legacy of £204 in recognition of benefits received, from the late Mr. Arthur Higgs of Ohio, who left the School as long ago as 1861 and emigrated to the U.S.A.".

"The Governors have recently considered the question of summer clothing for the boys and have decided to equip them with blazers and shorts."

In May a special meeting was called to consider an offer for the site of £115,000 but the negotiations were short lived and came to nothing. It seemed as though every meeting brought the report of a proposed offer or the hint of an offer about to be made.

1926

By the early part of the year, the Governors were hoping to sell the old site fairly soon and were concerned about re-housing the School in the likely interval between the sale and the completion of the new School. A temporary solution was available in the shape of Hints Hall, Tamworth which was offered at a rent of £225 per annum for three years, but was found to be unsuitable when visited by the body of Governors. They were more impressed by Canwell Hall. A temporary move of this kind was seen however, as no more than emergency planning and for the most part the attention of the Governing body was focussed on the certain move to the Harborne site when the right conditions prevailed. With this in mind, it had been established that the Calthorpe Estate was willing to sell a further 7¼ acres of freehold land, adjacent to the 17 acres already acquired, for £2,250. In June the School's Solicitors, Messrs. Smythe, Etches & Co were instructed to conclude the deal.

At the same time, a report from a sub-committee had been accepted, dealing with the future policy of the School. Concise as the report was, it outlined nevertheless the direction that the School should follow and the probable building requirements at Harborne, when circumstances allowed.

1927

In April a written offer of £120,000 for the school site was received from the Birmingham City Engineer & Surveyor. Equally as welcome as this offer from the City Council, was the closing sentence of the letter:

"Further it is understood that you remain as tenants at a rental until such time as you are able to move to your new premises".

Although the consent of the Board of Education had to be sought and the usual formalities dealt with, the situation was such that the Governors could report to subscribers:

"The Governors are actively proceeding with the scheme for the new School on the Harborne site and have appointed as joint architects Mr. J.L. Ball and Mr. H.W. Simister. . . . It has been decided to abandon the idea of one large building and to erect in place thereof, houses for the children with educational and administrative blocks".

(Mr. Ball and Mr. Simister had both submitted plans in the 1913 competition and had been placed first and second by the assessors). By November, the sale of the Colmore Row site had been completed and under the terms of the sale, the School could continue to occupy the premises until December 1930 if necessary, at an annual rental of £5,000. The land at Olton, bought originally as the intended new site for the School, had been sold profitably and a legacy of £1,000 had been received from the will of Mr. Lewis S. Richards. So the year closed on a note of optimism. The old site had at last been sold for a good price that would cover the cost of building a new and modern school on the desirable site at Harborne, even after allowing for the rental due to the Council for the continued occupation of the old building. Also, without doubt, the new School was to be built at the right time, when the costs of building were at their lowest. It would seem that, in the end, the long interval between the first proposal to transfer the School and the realisation of this proposal, some fifty-five years, had in fact worked to the advantage of the School.

1928

Understandably the Governors were anxious to move matters as quickly as possible to the point where the building work could start at Harborne. Outline plans for the School had been drawn up already, though there were some minor revisions made, but detailed plans had to be prepared by the architects and, when these had been agreed by the Governors, the approval of the Calthorpe Estate and the Board of Education had to be obtained. It was, in fact, the end of the year before the plans were completed and passed to the Quantity Surveyors, Messrs. Silk & Frazier, for costing. Meanwhile the Committee was not allowed to forget the day to day affairs of the School. In January a recommendation was accepted that hairbrushes should be provided for the boys and the tender of Messrs. Thos. Goode Ltd. of 30s. per dozen was approved, subject to the brushes being of British manufacture.

In November a proposal was received from Mr. Allen, who had, in December 1927, replaced Mr. Irving as Headmaster. The proposal was to take the whole school, boys, girls and staff to Morfa Holiday Camp, Conway for a two week holiday in June 1929. The scheme met with the full approval of the Governors, who authorised a booking for the first fortnight of June 1929, subject to "confirmation after inspection". The costs of this marvellous opportunity for the children were:

Fares   170 at 7s. 6d; 10 at 15s.;   £71.   5s.   0d.
Accommodation 170 at 37s.;   10 at 60s.; £344. 10s.   0d.

So, the whole school could travel to North Wales, be accommodated and fed for two weeks, for £415. 15s. 0d.!

1929

Work on the construction of roads at the Harborne site was started in February and the contract for the general building work was placed in May. The costs of these two contracts amounted to £81,000 and excluded, at this stage, the Chapel, but the Building Committee was asked to reserve the sum of £10,000 to cover the cost of this building and later in the year the architects were required to submit plans for approval. It was always intended that the Chapel should be built at the earliest possible moment in order to express the Christian ethic that was central to the school's philosophy. Initially, however, the most urgent need was to ensure the completion on time of the areas for education, accommodation and administration.

The year also brought a glimpse of problems concerning the framework and purpose of the school that were to recur with increasing frequency, as the system of national education was examined and revised, (it's still happening of course) to meet the expectations and demands of the nation. The Hadow Report had been published, recommending to the Board of Education the reorganisation of all public elementary schools. After some consideration, a small party of Governors — George Bryson (Chairman), Bishop Hamilton Baynes, Sir James Curtis, Alderman A.H. James, and Mr. F.H. Viney — was chosen to consult with the officials at the Board of Education in London.

As far as the pupils were concerned, however, the main news of the year was that the school camp at Conway had been highly successful.

1930

No doubt there was great excitement among the pupils when the Governors agreed in January to a further summer camp, though stipulating that this was not to be seen as an annual commitment, once the move to Harborne had been made. The Chairman was able to report to the March meeting that the deputation had met the Board of Education's representatives and had come away

> "convinced that the proper course to adopt is to organise the new school as a Senior School, although it will be necessary for a time to have a junior class for children admitted or about to be admitted under the age of 11".

The Governors accepted the inevitable and resolved that the new school should open as a Senior School. By July there was considerable anxiety as to whether the new school buildings

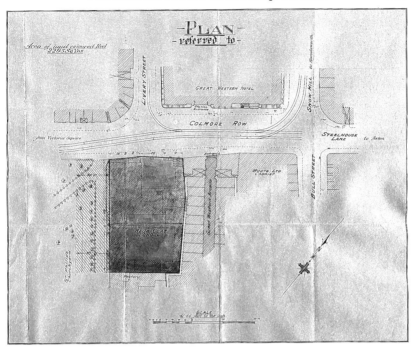

Plan of the site sold to the City Council.

would be available for the start of the new school year, as had been expected. A number of Governors had inspected the buildings and were convinced that there was no possibility that they would be ready for occupation by September 8th, but at their meeting at the end of September:

> "The Secretary reported that the change over to the new buildings was made on the 5th inst. and that he handed over the keys of the old premises to the representative of the Corporation of Birmingham on the 29th inst".

> "Resolved that at this first meeting at the new school the Governors desire to record their appreciation of the work of the architects, Messrs. J.L. Ball and H.W. Simister and the builders Messrs. B.Whitehouse & Sons Ltd., who have produced an Institution worthy of its purpose".

For 206 years the boys and girls of the school had looked out across St. Philip's Place to the church and had shared, or been aware of, the continually increasing bustle of the life outside the walls of the school, as the young town developed into a city and the fields and orchards disappeared, to be remembered only as names. No doubt some nostalgia was felt for the familiar surroundings of the Colmore Row site, but their new situation, in fine, purpose built houses with playing fields just outside the door and ample room to play and explore, must have delighted the pupils.

Wednesday October 29th was fixed as the day on which the Chairman of Governors, George A.Bryson J.P. (a Governor since 1913 and Chairman since 1919) would officially open the New School.

Blue Coat School Boys in 1910.
Left to right: John Hough, Wilfred Brown, Ernest Tofield,
Wilfred Bloor, Tom Chapman, William Herbert, Bernard Hack,
Arthur Hancox, Joseph Hinsley, Clinton Tye, Leslie Stone,
Reginald Hobby.

14

1931 – 1950
Some Difficult Years at Harborne

The move to Harborne had overcome an urgent need. No longer the hostage of the city centre, the school could stretch itself and feel at ease in the unaccustomed luxury of the acres of green and pleasant surroundings that were now its new home. One of the major planning decisions had been to build five separate Houses, three for the boys named St. Philip's, St. Martin's and St. George's (it was intended originally to call the latter St. Bartholomew's) and two for the girls — St. Monica's and St. Margaret's. This division of the pupils into smaller home units than they had known previously, each House being looked after by a lady Superintendent, offered a closer approximation to family life than had been possible in the old school. Now thirty to forty pupils could learn to live together in one building and develop loyalties to their House.

The future seemed very promising, but inside a decade the second world war was in progress. The years that followed the end of this six year war brought social changes and a series of new problems that presented a serious challenge to the school and for a few years deprived it of the proud independence which it had been able to maintain for over two hundred years. Fortunately the school was no less loyally and ably supported during these difficult years by its Governors, administrators and subscribers than it had been since its foundation. The present status of the school is a good indication of the patient and capable management with which it was guided through this period.

The improvement in social conditions which had begun slowly in the 1930s, had halted for the duration of the war but afterwards accelerated towards the Welfare State, posed the first major problem. If not in practice, then by definition, charitable institutions were anomalies in the prevailing, political outlook.

Their continued existence was threatened for a time, either nationally or locally, by the social and political dogma that sought to re-shape British society. For the same reasons, and for the first time in its history, the school also found that the number of children of the type for which it had been founded and for whom it had provided for over two centuries, was dwindling. The long negotiations with the Charity Commission, resulting in the 1895 Scheme of Government, had preserved the right of the school to continue its work without interference. New circumstances were now weakening its primary function.

There were new ideas and practices also in education. For a long time the school had provided an admirable standard of education, often practising what others merely preached. Science and French had been brought into the curriculum before the end of the nineteenth century; swimming instruction and physical education had been regular features for many years. The calibre of the pupils it had produced and the reports of frequent inspections testified to the progressive ideas followed by the school. Now, however, the national machinery for education began to hum more dynamically. The 1928 Hadow Report and the 1944 Education Act required of all schools higher standards and greater efficiency.

Finally there was the considerable problem of the steeply rising costs of running the school, which pulled expenditure above income with regular insistence. Annual costs per boarder were given as:

> 1905: £ 23. 10s. 0d. all inclusive.
> 1948: £116.   0s. 0d. ⎰ excluding educational
> 1959: £245.   0s. 0d. ⎱ expenses

By 1949 it became necessary to realise £16,000 of invested money, which reduced the accumulated deficiency but had the obvious consequence of reducing income also. War damage between 1939 and 1945, to property and estates owned by the school, reduced the annual income from this source for many years. The dilemma was that the school operated uneconomically unless all the places were filled, but it was becoming increasingly difficult to find the money to support a full school. A partial remedy was applied to this situation by the introduction of voluntary contributions from the parents or sponsors of children in the school, where this was an appropriate charge. During these years too, the school benefited from a considerable number of legacies and generous donations, which made it possible to keep the buildings and grounds well maintained and to extend the amenities.

The difficulties outlined above, brought about some changes. Like many old institutions, the school had to choose between a rigid adherence to its old system, or a recognition of the altered circumstances in which it was operating. In effect, there was no real alternative but to adapt itself to the changing times, if it was to retain purpose and vigour.

1932

"After careful consideration of the Hadow Report on the re-organisation of schools, the Governors resolved that the school generally be considered a senior school for children of 11+ and the curriculum arranged accordingly, with a junior department for children aged 9 to 11."

By October the school Chapel was completed, at a total cost, including the fees of the architects — Messrs Ball and Simister — of £7,323. The Chapel was duly dedicated on the 23rd November by the Rt. Reverend the Lord Bishop of Birmingham, Dr. E.W. Barnes. Since then, many hundreds of pupils, staff and parents have enjoyed its pleasant and peaceful atmosphere.

1933

In the Hall of the old school in Colmore Row, lists of benefactors were printed on wooden panels. When the school moved to Harborne these boards were removed with the intention of re-locating them but no suitable site could be agreed. The Governors thought "these panels were out of keeping with the new buildings". Eventually Miss Margery Francis was asked to transfer the information into a *Book of Benefactions*. She completed this work in April and then the old boards were destroyed. The book is kept in a case in the main entrance Hall of the Administration block. It is well worth looking through as a reminder of the generosity of the school's benefactors.

1934

An order was placed for boys' school suits. These were three piece, all wool Cheviot serge, indigo dyed and cost £1. 4s. 0d. By a contract made at the same time, milk was supplied to the school at 1s. 1d. a gallon.

1935

"In September the children gave their fifth broadcast service from the Birmingham Parish Church. They sang five hymns and Phyllis Hudson, aged fourteen, read the lesson. A large number of letters was received giving unstinted praise for the children's singing from all parts of Great Britain, and one from France".

"The Governors acknowledge with grateful thanks receipt of £1,000 from Sir William Waters Butler, Bart., to commemorate the late Mr. W. Owen Butler's connection with the school. . . . The amount has been invested and a Scholar-

A workman holding the plaque about to be put on the wall of the Prudential Building in Colmore Row.

ship to be called the'William Owen Butler Scholarship' has been founded."

1936

There were 164 children in the school and the decision was taken to reduce the age of admission from 9 years to 7 years. The school Medical Officer refuted the suggestion that too much starchy food in the school diet was the cause of boils. He stated that the diet was a good one and in no way responsible for any disorders. The doctor went on to say that the worst feature in the school was constipation among the children, and to advise that a good drink of water every morning before breakfast and another before dinner would be useful. His advice was passed on to the Lady Superintendents of the Houses.

1937

The President, Sir Charles Hyde, suggested that the new owners of the old B.C.S site should be asked for permission to record that the school stood there for over 200 years. The Prudential Assurance Company agreed to the request and the plaque, familiar to many of Birmingham's citizens, was mounted on the wall of the Prudential building. It had been made by Messrs. Doulton & Co of Lambeth.

Two coronation oaks, presented by Mr. Viney, were planted and added to the already impressive collection of trees, shrubs and flowers that made the school grounds so pleasant.

1939

The declaration of war on September 3rd obliged the Governors to act urgently on the matter of providing air raid shelters. Five were built, with lighting and seating, on the back field. They are still there, as overflow storage areas. Also St. Margaret's House was in effect commandeered as sleeping accommodation for nurses and medical students from Queen Elizabeth Hospital.

1940   October.

"The Secretary reported that this morning he was approached by Mrs. Bindley, Chairman of the Governors of Crowley's Orphanage, Lee Crescent, Edgbaston, who asked if the Governors would admit their fourteen girls, age 7 to 14. It was imperative to secure accommodation at once as the premises had become unsafe owing to recent and intense enemy action".

The girls were admitted immediately.

December.

The Governors took the decision to keep all the children at school during the Christmas holiday (December 18th – 30th), considering they would be safer there than at home.

1941

Mr. Allen (Headmaster) resigned in February and the Governors took two curious decisions. The first was to make Miss Ward acting Head for educational matters but to transfer ultimate authority for the time being to the Secretary, Mr. J.E. Hall. The second was to offer the appointment of Headmaster to the Reverend R.J.C. Gutteridge, a former Chaplain of the school.

By the time of their April meeting however, the Governors had learned that the proposed appointment of the Reverend Gutteridge as Headmaster, could not be approved by the Board of Education. They had their own way. The Reverend Gutteridge was appointed Principal and Chaplain of the school and occupied the Headmaster's house, while Mr. E.F. Lloyd, a serving member of the staff, was made acting Headmaster and Superintendent of St. Martin's House. Strange situations arise in wartime, and sometimes strange solutions have to be applied!

1942

"For some years Mr. F.H.Viney has been good enough to give £1 for every boy or girl who retains his or her situation for two years after leaving the school. He has now decided very generously to put his scheme on a permanent basis and he has presented £500 to provide an annual income to continue the scheme." Over the thirteen years that the scheme had operated already, 183 former pupils had received this award.

At the same meeting, Mr. and Mrs. F.E. Pearson notified the school that they intended to finance an award which they wished to be given chiefly for initiative and enterprise. This became known as the Offley Wade Scholarship. The first recipient was Derek Hopkins, an apprentice with Dale Forty and Co.

1943

"Miss Edith Barling has given to the school a portrait of her grandfather, Henry Edmunds, who was a scholar at the Blue Coat School 1811 – 1817. He became Managing Director of the Birmingham and Midland Bank, New Street, Birmingham."

"Mr. Edward Jefferson has given a portrait of his father, Frederick Thomas Jefferson J.P. who was also a scholar, 1864 – 1868. He was Chairman of Messrs. Kenrick & Jefferson Ltd., 1900 – 1920 and Chairman of the Britannic Assurance Co. Ltd., 1897 – 1920."

There is uncertainty about the present whereabouts of these two portraits.

1945   March.

The Reverend Gutteridge resigned from his post as Principal. No replacement was sought. Mr. Lloyd moved in to the house vacated by the Reverend Gutteridge and resumed the traditional role of the Headmaster, that of running the school.

Nominations and applications for places in the school were being received in steady numbers. In June 1945 there were ten applications, nineteen in September, thirteen in December and ten in March 1946, making a total for the year of fifty-two, of whom forty-three were admitted.

1946

The position of the school under the 1944 Education Act was causing the Governors some concern. A special meeting in March considered a preliminary report, following an informal approach to the Local Education Authority about the future of the school. It was decided to appoint a Re-organisation Committee to look further into the matter. By the end of July, the Governors learned that at a meeting at the City Council House earlier in the month:

> "It was generally agreed that the only line to take was for the school to become a voluntary aided primary school for 320 children of ages 7 to 11+."

The management of this proposed school would consist of one third L.E.A. representatives, and two thirds Blue Coat School representatives. The Governors learned also that the council was interested in acquiring part of the Blue Coat School site, with a view to building a new secondary school there.

At this same meeting the Governors paid tribute to their colleague, Mr. G.A. Bryson, who had died at the beginning of the month. George Bryson C.B.E., J.P., had been Chairman of Governors for 27 years (1919 – 1946) and had guided the development of the school with great ability. A Bryson Memorial Fund was opened to provide a Bursary or Scholarship.

1947

A meeting was held in April at the Ministry of Education, at which the Ministry officials, the Birmingham Chief Education Officer and the party of Governors, agreed to the proposed change in the status of the school, the Governors being required to apply to the L.E.A. for the school to become maintained as soon as possible.

1948

By the end of July, Birmingham Education Committee had formally accepted the Blue Coat School as a Voluntary Aided Primary School as from 1st. September 1948 and this was confirmed by the Ministry of Education in November. In brief, the main effects of this move were:

1. The Governors were relieved of educational expenses, text books, all teaching materials and teachers' salaries, as well as maintenance and decoration of classrooms. All these expenses became the responsibility of the Birmingham Education Department.

2. Day pupils could now be admitted to the school at the discretion of the local education authority.

3. The Headmaster, Mr. Lloyd, became an employee of the L.E.A.

4. The boarding side of the school was not affected. This remained under the sole control of the Governors and the expenses of running the Houses was of course, a charge on the Endowment Fund. The Blue Coat uniform was worn only by the Boarding Foundationers.

Negotiations were still in progress over the sale of about seven acres of the school grounds to the Birmingham Education Committee, as a site for a new Secondary Modern School, and the school Auditors had declared a deficit for the year of £6,700 — a modest sum by today's standards, but a not inconsiderable amount at that time, since the cost per boarder (excluding educational expenses) was £116.

1950

The appointment of Mr. G.G.F. Greig as Warden, with effect from mid-August was approved. He occupied the house vacated by Mr. Lloyd, and became responsible to the Governors for the well being of the Blue Coat boarders and for "the day to day running of the institution". This did not include the school and all educational matters which were the province of Mr. Lloyd and the Local Education Authority.

The changed status of the school and the consequent transfer to the Local Education Authority of all the expenses of the school, infringed the original purposes of the Charity — to maintain and educate the children in their charge. Yet, so far as can be ascertained, this attracted no protest or accusation that the aims of the foundation were being abandoned, or modified in order to meet the changed circumstances of the time. When, however, the Governors decided to regain control of the school and tackle the problems in a different way, the reaction was one of indignant and immediate hostility, as we shall see.

15

1951 – 1967
Re-organisation Proposals
Encounter Opposition but Finally
the School Prospers

Well aware that they had not yet found a medium to long term solution to the financial problems of the Institution, and also far from being reconciled to losing control of the school permanently, the Governing body asked its executive committee to consider and report on the possibilities for re-organising the Foundation. In their deliberations, this committee had to accept a number of factors and circumstances:

1. The institution was no longer a unity as it had been until recently.

2. The charity was overspending each year to the tune of two to three thousand pounds.

3. Endowment income was approximately £14,000 per annum and the cost of maintaining and educating a pupil was nearing £200.

4. The buildings could accommodate 150 boarders but the income could support only seventy.

5. There was school provision for 200 pupils.

So, in the Annual Report for 1952 this statement appeared:

"In a recent interview with the Ministry of Education, who act in this matter for the Charity Commission, it was clearly established that the Foundation had become outmoded and a major scheme of re-organisation must be undertaken to bring the Charity in line with modern conditions."

The School Governors were not, of course, free agents. They were bound to operate the charity within the provisions of the scheme agreed with the Charity Commissioners in 1895, (see chapter 11), and could not alter the operation of the charity without first securing the agreement of the Ministry of Education, acting on behalf of the Charity Commission. They were constrained also by the arrangement made with the Birmingham

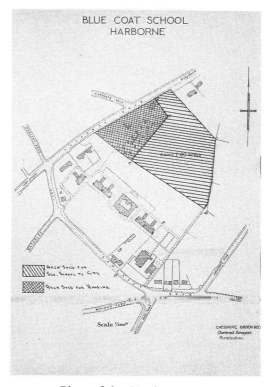

BLUE COAT SCHOOL
HARBORNE

Plan of the Harborne site.

Education Department, in 1948, whereby the school had become Voluntary Aided and was funded by that authority. Finally, though less obviously, the Governors realised that any changes to the framework in which the school operated, would need to be acceptable to those individuals for whom the school was a practical demonstration of society's concern for the less fortunate — subscribers, donors and ex-scholars. These individuals would almost certainly look at any proposed changes with caution.

By the middle of 1952, the Governing Body was considering a proposal that would convert the school into a boarding and day preparatory school for 200 pupils, some thirty of whom would be Foundationers, maintained and educated by the income from the endowment funds. The others would be fee payers. Discussion of this proposal brought in the resignation of the Warden, Mr. Greig, who objected to the notion of fee payers. (He was replaced by Mr. C. Trenchard, appointed for two years). Although nothing was as yet decided or agreed, moves were made in anticipation of a change in the school's status. As boarders left, their places were not filled and consequently there was a gradual fall in the number of foundationers. It was also clear to the Governors that they would need to regain control of the school from the local authority and preliminary action was taken to effect this. Not unnaturally the Birmingham Education authority felt some concern about the speed with which the school was preparing to abandon its Voluntary Aided status, so soon after this had been granted.

A conference at the school in June 1953, between representatives of the Ministry, the L.E.A. and the Governors, had the result that a revised scheme was prepared and circulated. This limited the age range to pupils between 7 and 11 years and while proposing to give preference to children of Birmingham, envisaged that any remaining places could be filled with applicants from outside the city areas. Until now, knowledge of the proposed changes had been restricted but it was inevitable that information about them would reach a wider public. This happened in December 1953. A slightly bemused public found that the affairs of the Blue Coat School were now rarely absent from their local newspapers, whether as headlined articles, letters, or editorial comment. This continued for several years as the Governors of the school and those who supported the proposed changes, attempted to inform the public and to counter the claims and assertions of the opponents of the scheme.

The scheme's opponents were a number of former scholars of the school and some local politicians. The objections of this group were to the proposed limitation of the age range (7 – 11), to the idea that any of the children in the school would be fee payers, and to the extension of the charity beyond the city limits. Their objections were eventually set out in a petition to the Queen. Despite the pressure, the Governors gave notice, in August 1955, of their intention to abandon Voluntary Aided status and to re-gain control of the school by September 1956. They clearly expected that the scheme would have received approval and would be operative by that date. The post of Headmaster was advertised and Mr. B.C. Faulds was appointed to take up his position in May and to prepare to re-open the Foundation in September. Meanwhile the Local Education Authority had made arrangements to transfer the day pupils to neighbouring schools.

When the school assembled for the start of the Christmas Term 1956, all the pupils were Blue Coats, but there were only twenty-one of them, seventeen boys and four girls. The proposed scheme had been blocked by the tactics of the dissenting group, and the Ministry had declared itself unwilling to proceed in view of the strength of the opposition.

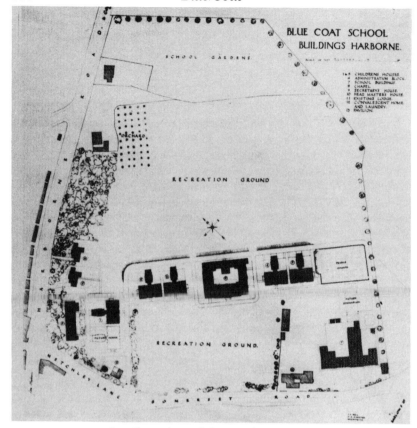

Another plan of the Harborne site.

More months of consultation and negotiation followed. At the end of May 1957, a delegation from the Ministry of Education visited the school and a month later, at the end of June, a conference was held at the Ministry in London, at which all interested parties, including the objectors, were represented. None of these manoeuvres produced harmony or a solution and accordingly the Ministry now informed the Governors that it would not be possible to implement the scheme. Faced with this check to their plans, the Governors decided that their wisest course of action was to administer the school under the old 1895 scheme. For six years they had endeavoured without success to replace it with a scheme more suitable to the second half of the twentieth century. Now the school needed a period of stability in which to grow to an economic size and to re-affirm its traditional values.

An enormous amount of time and energy had been expended, only to arrive back at the point of departure — the 1895 scheme.

It was not all wasted effort however. The school and its affairs had received a great deal of publicity and was known now to a wider public than previously. There was too a better understanding of its aims, its financial problems, and of the adjustments that would have to be made. Another gain was that the link between the school and former scholars of the school appeared to have strengthened. Whether they had opposed or supported the scheme for re-organisation, former scholars realised now that their continued interest and support were important to the school's well being.

Following a visit of H.M. Inspectors of Schools in October 1957, the school was granted provisional recognition by the Ministry of Education, a vital step in its rehabilitation. After a further inspection in November 1960, full recognition was granted. The number of pupils rose steadily each year. In September 1961 there were ninety-eight boys and twenty-eight girls. By April 1966 the number of pupils in Main School was 169. Of these 107 were full boarders, thirteen were weekly boarders and forty-nine were day pupils. Additionally, there were sixty-seven pupils in the pre-preparatory department, opened in 1965 in St. Margaret's House for 4 – 7 year old day pupils.

Some of the interesting items of these years are shown below.

1958

A very generous donation of £8,000 was received from an anonymous donor, who specified that the money was to be added to the Bursary Fund and used to pay the full costs or the part costs of extra pupils.

1959

A Governor offered £500 per year for the next three years, to help with the cost of re-opening St. George's House. It was decided to admit up to fifty day pupils at a charge of £25 per term. This move was made with Ministry approval, as there was an excess of classroom accommodation over that required by the boarding foundationers. Voluntary contributions from parents or sponsoring bodies were introduced. The contribution, at maximum, was the difference between the full cost per pupil of £234 per annum and the £110 provided by the endowment income. In cases of need, the Bursary Fund was used to meet the costs of any pupil.

1961

Mr. and Mrs. Viney donated £10,000 to the Bursary Fund. An appeal organised by Mr. Viney had brought in further contributions to this fund and two former scholars (Miss Rose Bridgwater,

1890 – 1895, now living in America; Mr. Albert Bridgwater, 1895 – 1898, now living in Canada) had written to say that they had decided to come to England in order to visit the school and donate £1,000.

1962

A portrait of Mr. F.H.Viney (by Miss Dawn Cookson) was completed and was hung in the Board Room.

1963

The new staff houses for the Housemasters of the three boys' houses were completed and occupied, and Mr. Viney made a further gift to the Bursary Fund of £3,000.

1965

St. Margaret's House, which had been let to Birmingham Corporation since 1959 and used as accommodation for trainee teachers, was recovered and opened as a Pre-Preparatory Department. Its success was immediate, and two years later it had ninety-eight pupils.

1966

Mr. Viney gave notice of his intention to resign from the Board of Governors. He had served the school for forty-five years and was granted the title of Honorary Life Governor as a mark of appreciation of his work and generosity.

1967

The Venerable S. Harvie Clark, Archdeacon of Birmingham, resigned from the Board of Governors after twenty years as the Board's Chairman. He too was granted the title of Honorary Life Governor, in recognition of his service to the school. His dedication and leadership had been of real value during a difficult period.

The last note for this year takes us back to the foundation of the school. In October the Governors were advised that:

"The Bank of England (Temple Row, Birmingham) was reported to have requested the cancellation, in consideration of a capital payment, of the annual payment of £2 made to the Governors since 1729 under the will of Thomas Dunscombe."

The payment was extinguished for the sum of £100. How much better it would have been, to have retained this unique link to the first days of the school, rather than sever it so cheaply after 238 years.

16

1968 – 1990
Heading for the Twenty-first Century

At the Annual General Meeting in March 1968, the Chairman of Governors, Mr. P.A.G. Osler, referred to "the thriving, unified Preparatory School of today". Bearing in mind the difficulties the school had faced, only thirteen years previously, this was a welcome statement, confirming the advances made during those years. In the two decades covered by this last chapter, these advances have been continued as the school has expanded its facilities, modernised its buildings and equipment and rationalised its structure. In effect the school has had to prepare itself to enter the twenty-first century as a strong and efficient unit, responsive to the needs and demands of the time, without losing its individual character or separating itself from the traditional values that it has always upheld. Simply carrying the name Blue Coat will be no guarantee of success in a society that focuses more on the present and the future than on the past.

The period contains two significant events for the school. The first of these was the sale in 1983, to the city of Birmingham, of an area of land in Sparkbrook, approximately 49 acres, on which stood several hundred properties, residential and commercial. From this sale the school acquired a considerable capital sum to invest (just over £2 million) and from the investment, an annual income that allowed a programme of modernisation and improvements to be undertaken. A lot of this work passes unnoticed — re-wiring, re-roofing, more efficient heating plants, updating the main kitchen facilities etc. Some of it is more obvious, particularly to ex-boarders looking with disbelief at the warm, carpeted dormitories of their old Houses. They must shake their heads in amazement at the absence of draughts and the disappearance of the rather spartan conditions they had known.

The other significant event was the agreement between the Governing Body of the school and the Charity Commission on a new scheme to replace the 1895 scheme under which the school was managed. When this was finally sealed, in March 1986, after many years of negotiations, the way forward for the school became much clearer. The new scheme recognised that the school was now a fee paying preparatory school for boarders and day pupils but that it had a strong charity component. It was stipulated that:

"The Governors shall set aside . . . a sum equal to not less than 10% of the total amount of the annual fee income of the Charity . . . and shall apply such sum in maintaining places at the school for children of merit, good character and sufficient health who by reason of orphanage or other adversity are in need of financial assistance."

These places are known as Foundation Places. Under the 1895 scheme Foundationers had to be boarders; the 1986 scheme made it possible for foundation places to be awarded to day pupils also. In both cases, preference has to be given to candidates from the city of Birmingham. Other provisions allowed the Governors to award Scholarships for merit and bursaries to pupils, or former pupils, in need of financial assistance.

No close study of the scheme is needed to realise that in some particulars the school's constitution has changed. The admission of fee payers is the most obvious example. There is also a clause in the new scheme that prohibits the withholding from a pupil of any advantage or emolument on the grounds that the pupil is exempted from attending religious instruction and chapel services, i.e. is not Church of England. The need for change may cause some regret; most people would probably accept, however, that the changes made represent a sensible and realistic solution to the school's situation. It could not allow itself to be trapped in its own past, however fine and meritorious that past had been.

The following notes, some dealing with matters of general interest and others with developments over the last twenty years, bring this account of the school up to date.

1970

The Society of Friends of the Blue Coat School held an inaugural meeting. Later referred to as the Association of Friends, its members have raised remarkable amounts of money to finance a number of important projects, the biggest of which was the swimming pool.

1972

Chosen as the year to celebrate the 250th anniversary of the school. An illustrated booklet was produced, containing a resumé of the growth of the school and a commemoration service was held in Birmingham Cathedral. Then, in July, the school was visited by Prince William of Gloucester, who was to die only six weeks later.

1974

The plastic dome over the pool had been destroyed in a gale early in 1973. The Association of Friends now decided, with the support of the governing body, to launch an appeal to provide a permanent cover.

The orchard and spinney area, fronting Harborne Road (2.4 acres) was sold very profitably (£104,000) for a housing scheme. A new Library and two additional classrooms, in a single pre-fabricated block, were brought into use at the end of October.

1975

Mr. R.L.Ekin resigned from the Governing Body which he had served since 1937. In September the permanent structure over the pool was completed.

1976

Mr. C.G. Marsh retired at the end of July, after fifty-four years as groundsman to the school. The school garden at the back of St. Martin's, St. George's and the Administration Block, was converted to an extra playing field.

1978

There were now two former pupils of the school serving as Governors — Mr. K.B. Purnell and Mr. B.L. Silvey. Both had had successful careers and the latter was elected to serve as President of the Foundation at the annual general meeting in March.

Financially it had not been a good year. The effects of inflation brought a forecast deficit for the Michaelmas Term of £17,000.

1979

Mr. B.C. Faulds retired and was succeeded in September by the present Headmaster, Mr. B.P. Bissell.

1980

A start was made on the installation of the large 1908 Norman and Beard organ bought from St. Wulstan's Church, Bournbrook. At the same time a programme of refurbishment and redecoration of the Chapel was put in hand. It was March 1982 before the Chapel could be used.

1983

The sale to the City of Birmingham of the Sparkbrook estate was completed.

Figures for this year show how the shape of the school could alter in a matter of years.

1977 — 136 Boarders: 80 day pupils: 67 pre-prep pupils
1983 — 69 Boarders: 139 day pupils: 120 pre-prep pupils

1984

Reflecting the investment of the money from the Sparkbrook sale, income for this year rose to £208,000 as opposed to £94,000 for the year 1982. This allowed a considerable expansion of the maintenance work and of improvements, notably the extension and modernisation of all four boarding houses, each house being closed in turn for six months during the renovations.

1986

The 1985 scheme was replaced, giving the school greater flexibility in a number of matters.

1988

Construction was started in July of a new Science, Art and Library building, known as the Centenary Building, to mark the 100th anniversary of Birmingham as a city. The building, which cost £½ million, was completed in May of the following year. An appeal was launched to meet the costs of equipping the new rooms and brought in £50,000.

The brochure showing the design of the Centenary Building and detailing the equipment required for the new rooms, has on the inside cover the catchphrase "We've come a long way since 1722".

That's an undeniable statement and one which implies, with good reason, pride in the present status and future prospects of the school. It also contains an echo from the past of harder days, a feeling for what has gone before, to make the present possible. That's how it should be.

Appendix A

Orders to be observed by the Master and Mistress in the Government of the Charity Schools in Birmingham

1. That they constantly attend the School in the Summer Half-year froɯ the hours of 7 in the morning till Morning Prayers and from 5 in the Evening till Evening Prayers, in the Winter Half-year from 8 till Morning Prayers and from 5 till Evening Prayers.

2. That they Teach the Children the true Spelling of Words make them mind their stops and bring them to read slowly and distinctly.

3. That the Boys be taught to write a fair legible hand with the grounds of Arithmetick. And that the Girls be taught to knitt sew and mend their cloaths to spin or any other work used in the place where they live to fitt them for services and apprentiships.

4. That they make it their chief business to instruct the Children in the principles of the Christian religion as professed and taught in the Church of England and laid down in the Church Catechism.

5. That they take particular care of the manners and behaviour of the Poor Children and by all propper methods discourage and correct the beginnings of vice such as lying swearing etc.

6. That they bring the Children to Church every Lords Day and every other day to prayers and instruct them to behave themselves there with all reverence and to joyn in the Publick Service with the Minister with an audible united and humble or low voice.

7. That they pray morning and evening in the School and teach the Children to do the same at home when they rise and goe to bed as also to say grace before and after meat the prayers to be collected out of the Publick Prayers of the Church or other forms to be approv'd of by the Minister.

8. That the Childrens names be called over every morning and evening and if any be missing to be put down with notes for tardy or absent and for great faults as lying swearing stealing truanting etc that they be noted down

in monthly or weekly bills to be laid before the subscribers or trustees every time they meet in order to correction or expulsion.

9. That the Children be permitted to break up at the three Great Festivals and no oftner.

10. That the Children wear their caps cloaths and bands every day whereby the trustees and benefactors may know them and see their behaviour when abroad.

2nd November 1722 at a solemn meeting then held by the then subscribers to the Charity School.

These orders were then made agreed upon and signed by us whose names are hereunder written being all or the major part of such persons as were then present subscribing a guinea a year each (the rest of the subscribers of a guinea a year each having had due notice of such meeting).

William Higgs; Richard Banner; John Williams; Randolph Bradburne; John Holtham; John Mander[*]; Nehemiah Tonkcs; William Weaman; Edward Ward; John Sale; Will Weeley; Walter Tippin; John Wood; John Savage; Thomas Duncombe.

---

[*] The John Mander who signed the 1722 Orders is almost certainly the one referred to in this notice from *Aris's Gazette* of May 18th 1747:

'To be Lett, a very good house, with proper Outbuilding, Gardening, Yard and other conveniences thereto belonging, situate in New Street Birmingham and now in the occupation of Mr. John Mander.'

Appendix B

Rules to be observed by the Trustees and Subscribers to the Charity Schools in Birmingham.

1. That they meet the first Friday in every month and what shall be agreed upon at such meetings by the majority shall be observed totomente from this day.

2. That the place of such meetings shall be fixed by the Chairman who shall be chosen by the Chairman present before 9 of the clock.

3. That the Trustees (one of which shall be Treasurer) shall be annually chosen, which with the Rectors of each Parish shall have the immediate care and government of the said schools.

4. That the nomination of such Children as are to be cloathed and taught shall be in them.

5. That the Trustees or Governors be chosen or nominated at the first meeting after Lady Day.

6. To prevent disputes in this election, every subscriber shall take his turn according as his name stands subscribed in the book.

7. That the Trustees shall choose a Treasurer out of their own body.

8. That the Treasurer shall receive what money is in stock, or shall at any time be paid in for the benefitt of the said schools.

9. That he lay out the same as shall be ordered by the majority at any of the meetings.

10. That in case of death the money so received may not be lost the Treasurer (if required) shall give a note under his hand to three or more of the Trustees for what he shall receive.

11. That the Treasurer keep a fair account of all the receipts and disbursements for the view of all the subscribers.

12. That the Treasurer bring in his accounts once or oftner in a year to be audited by the Trustees the majority of which have power to examine and pass the same.

2nd November 1722 etc.

Appendix C

Rules and Orders to be given to the Parents at the admittance of the Children into the Charity School.

1. That the Children at the time of their admittance are clean and free from any infectious distemper.

2. That they freely submit them to be chastised for their faults and forbear coming to school on such occasions that the Master and Mistress be not discouraged in the performance of their duties.

3. That if they apprehend their Children are abused by immoderate correction or otherwise they shall make their complaint to the Governors at their weekly meeting in order to have the same redress't.

4. That they shall permit their Children to continue in the School until such time as the subscribers shall think convenient to dispose of them and not entice their Children away upon any pretence whatsoever.

5. That a copy of these orders be printed and given to the parents of such child they having first oblidged themselves thereto by subscribing an order made the 16th of November 1726 to consider at what age to admit either boys or girls and what age they shall not exceed before they are put out.

6. That no boy be admitted under nine years old nor continue beyond the age of fourteen and that no girl be admitted under nine years old nor continue beyond the age of fiveteen.

December 11th 1726. It was this day agreed that the Orders above shall be the Standing Orders of the School.

Wm. Higgs; John Mander; Hen. Carver; Rich. Carless; Neh.Tonkes; Richd. Banner.

Appendix D

The School Badge – introduced in 1962
(*see illustration on page 76*)

1. The gold and red background is taken from the arms of the City of Birmingham.

2. The band across the badge is for Bishop Edward Chandler, Bishop of Coventry and Lichfield in 1722.

3. The upper white cross represents the Church and is also from the arms of Lichfield.

4. The lower cross is the usual symbol used to represent St. Philip.

5. The blue border contains the title of the school and the date of the foundation.

6. The motto 'Grow in Grace' is from the second Epistle of St. Peter, chapter 3, verse 18.

Appendix E

Headmasters

1724 – 1727 John Symonds
1727 – 1736 John Cooper
1736 – 1763 John Cottrell
1764 – 1765 Samuel Whitehouse
1765 – 1768 Ambrose Hill
1768 – 1770 Thomas Chaddocke
1770 – 1772 James Meer
1772 – ?   Samuel Haye
 ? – ?   Mr. Kempson
1781 – 1785 R. Ireland
1785 – 1803 B. Line
1803 – 1815 Edward Jones
1816 – 1832 Henry Jones
1833 – 1840 Josiah Jacques
1840   William Wallis (April – October)
1840 – 1847 James Foster
1847 – 1850 George Kirkland
1851   Edmund Hall (February – September)
1851 – 1857 Robert Symonds
1857 – 1859 Mr. Taylor
1859 – 1865 Mr. Welch
1865 – 1893 George S. Dunn
1893   G. Gill (May – August)
1894 – 1900 John Irving (Re-appointed in 1912)
1901 – 1903 T.J. Turned
1903 – 1904 E.T. Philips
1904 – 1906 H. Cleave
1906 – ?   William Howes
1912 – 1927 John Irving
1927 – 1941 A. M. Allen
1941 – 1949 E. F. Lloyd
1941 – 1945 Reverend R.J.C. Gutteridge (Principal)
1949 – 1952 G. F. Greig (Warden)
1952 – 1956 C. Trenchard (Warden)
1956 – 1979 B. Craig Faulds
1979 –   Brian P. Bissell

Presidents, 1875 – 1991

1875	The Right Hon. The Earl of Dartmouth
1876	John Homer Chance, Esq.
1877	Sampson S. Lloyd, Esq, M.P.
1878	The Right Hon. The Lord Norton
1879	The Hon. A.C.G. Calthorpe

1880	The Right Hon. The Lord Lyttleton
1881	Edward Gem, Esq, J.P.
1882	The Right Hon. The Lord Windsor
1883	James Watson, Esq, J.P.
1884	The Most Hon. The Marquis of Hereford
1885	John Jaffay, Esq, J.P.
1887	T.H.G. Newton, Esq, High Sheriff
1888	John Dent Goodman, Esq, J.P.
1889	John S. Dugdale, Esq, K.C., M.P.
1890	Alex M. Chance, Esq, J.P.
1891	Philip Albert Muntz, Esq, M.P.
1892	C.A. Smith-Ryland, Esq, J.P.
1893	The Right Hon. The Earl of Dudley
1895	Sir James Sawyer, M.D., J.P.
1896	The Right Hon. The Earl of Warwick
1897	The Right Hon. The Lord of Calthorpe
1898	Sir Henry Wiggin, Bart
1899	The Right Hon. The Viscount Cobham
1900	The Right Hon. Jesse Collings, M.P.
1902	His Grace The Duke of Marlborough
1903	Lt.-Gen. The Hon. S.J. Gough-Calthorpe
1904	The Right Revd. The Lord Bishop of Birmingham, Dr. Charles Gore
1905	The Right Revd. The Lord Bishop of Manchester, Dr. E.A. Knox
1907	The Right Hon. The Viscount Morpeth, M.P.
1908	Sir Francis Lowe, M.P.
1910	Sir Benjamin Stone, M.P.
1914	Ald. Sir W.H. Bowater, J.P., Lord Mayor of Birmingham
1915	Ald. Neville Chamberlain, J.P., Lord Mayor of Birmingham
1916	The Right Hon. The Lord Mayor of Birmingham
1924	The Right Revd. The Lord Bishop of Birmingham, Dr. E.W. Barnes
1925	Sir Charles Hyde, Bart.
1943	Colonel Sir Bertram Ford, T.D., D.L., LL.D., F.C.A
1948	The Hon. Mr. Justice Finnemore
1951	Brig. Sir Richard Anstruther-Gough-Calthorpe, Bart., C.B.E., LL.D
1957	Professor Humphrey F. Humphreys, C.B.E., M.C., D.L., M.B.
1961	The Right Revd. The Lord Bishop of Birmingham, Dr. J.L. Wilson
1966	Ald. Stephen Lloyd, M.A.
1971	The Right Revd. The Lord Bishop of Birmingham, Laurence A. Brown, M.A.
1978	B.L. Silvey, Esq.
1984	Professor Edward A. Marsland, B.D.S., Ph.D., F.D.S.R.C.S, F.R.C.Path

Appendix F

Sources of Information

1. School Records:
   Minute Books of the Governing Body from 1722.
   Annual Reports.

2. Birmingham Reference Library:
   *Hole and Corner Work! An address to the people of
   Birmingham on the Peculation at the Blue Coat
   School.* 1835. J.Allday

   No. 390329

   *Publick Education, particularly in the Charity
   Schools.* 1724 Sermon at St. Philip's. T.Bisse

   No. 12394

   *Act to vest estates and property of the Blue Coat School
   in new trustees.* 1845

   No. 17838

   History of Birmingham 1819. Hutton

   *Charity Commissioners Report 1815 – 1839.
   Vol. XXXV Warwick*

   No. 461412

   Century of Birmingham Life. Langford

   No. 407886

   *Historical Account of the Blue Coat School 1724 –
   1784: 1724 – 1806: 1724 – 1817: 1724 – 1830*

   No. 71548

   Newspaper cuttings relating to the Blue Coat School
   collected by G. H. Osborne 1866 – 1905.

   No. 243127

   The Town Book 1723

   Copy of Dr. Richard Banner's Will

3. Birmingham Museum and Art Gallery:
   Illustrations and photographs of the school building.

The Architectural Medal. J. Taylor Lists John Ottley's 1824 Medal of Blue Coat School.

Papers relating to the building work of Mr. H. W Simister at the Somerset Road site dated 1928 – 1930.

4. Bodleian Library, Oxford:
   MS. Rawlinson J. fol.2 f.125. *Short biographical notes on Richard Banner.*

   MS. Oxf. dioc. papers e.19 p.118. Specimen of Banner's hand when ordained deacon on 30 May 1702.

5. St. Philip's Cathedral:
   Vestry records for early years of eighteenth century.
   Copy of 1722 lease.

6. Prudential Insurance (Estate Division):
   Land titles, plans and schedules of the Colmore Row site, inc. the 1722 indenture.

   1894 scheme for the administration of the school.

7. Other Sources:
   Our Birmingham published by Cadbury's.

   Aris's Gazette and the more recently founded newspapers.

Appendix G

Money Equivalents

Readers not familiar with pre-decimal currency and interested to establish the modern equivalents of amounts mentioned in the text, should note that:

1. A guinea or sovereign was twenty one shillings – £1.05.
2. A shilling, of which there were twenty to the £, represents 5p.
3. There were twelve pennies to the shilling.

Having made the conversion, readers should bear in mind the huge difference in value caused by inflation. A donation of £100 in 1900 would have a value at least fifty times greater today.

Measurements

1. There are roughly two and a half acres to the hectare.
2. A yard equals 90 centimetres. A foot equals 30 cms.

Glossary

Poage	: thick soup (French — *potage*)
Pease	: old spelling of peas
Porage	: a gruel.
	"If the porage be burned . . . or the meate overroasted, we say the bishop hath put his foote in the potte."
	(Tindale, *Obed, Christ Man*)
	"Till one, pease porrage, pottatoes and Apple Pye" (Susanne Darwin, *E Darwin's Life*)
Hasly	: meat loaf
Firmity	: strength — thought to be a humorous school name for something solid.
Moiety	: half (French — *moitié*)
Eleemosynary	: given in charity
Piggin	: drinking vessel, often of wood

Trencher   : wooden plate (French — *trenchoir*)
In modern English we still refer to a
hearty eater as a good trencherman.

Tipit   : (usual spelling 'tippet'). cloth covering for
the neck and shoulders worn by women
over a dress and by various officials as
part of their ceremonial duties, when it
was often made of fur.

Appendix H

Plans of the Colmore Row building. 1907

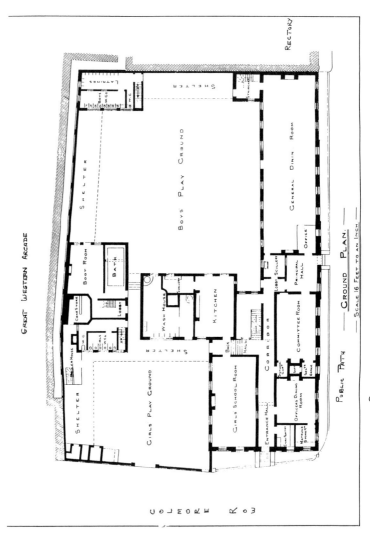

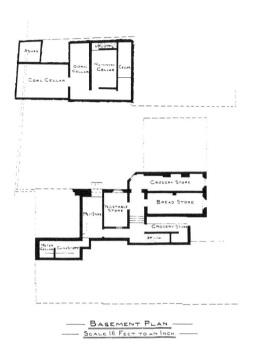

BASEMENT PLAN
SCALE 16 FEET TO AN INCH

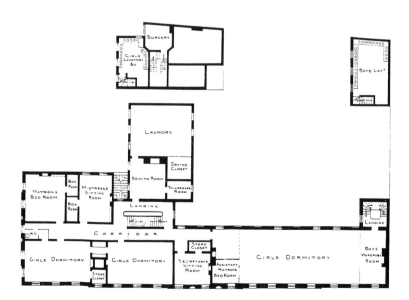

FIRST FLOOR PLAN.
SCALE 16 FEET TO AN INCH

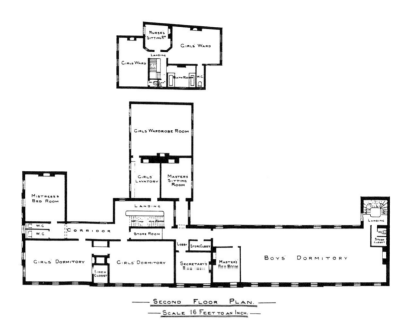

SECOND FLOOR PLAN.
SCALE 16 FEET TO AN INCH.

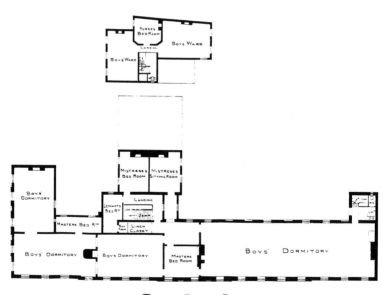

THIRD FLOOR PLAN.
SCALE 16 FEET TO AN INCH

Index